WATERBIRD
WINGS OVER WINDERMERE®

BY ANNE HUGHES & IAN GEE

Published by Anne Hughes and Ian Gee, 2023

Text: © Anne Hughes and Ian Gee, 2023
Photographs:
AH – Anne Hughes
IG – Ian Gee
LFC – Lakes Flying Company Ltd.
Photos marked ** in the captions courtesy of *Primetime Media Ltd.* with thanks to Steve White and Jo White.
Photos courtesy of *Air TV* with * with thanks to Ian Cundall.
Design: Trevor Jago
Print: Jump Design & Print
ISBN: 978-1-3999-4904-0

Any profits from the sale of this book will go to The Lakes Flying Company Ltd. Charity number 1138624

Main front cover image: Katie Hounsome

Lower images –
Top left: Lakes Flying Company Ltd.
Top right: Lakes Flying Company Ltd.
Bottom left: Mark Wright
Bottom right: Anne Hughes

Inside front cover: Avro Curtiss-type at Brooklands, by Stephen Chard GAvA

Back cover: Ray Troll

Inside back cover: Mark Wright

FOREWORD

It is hard to associate the silvan fells and the rippling waters of Windermere with the cutting edge of aviation. Yet, just over a century ago, the lake was host to the birth of a technology that went on to transform the world, the seaplane. Edward Wakefield's Waterbird was the first hydro-aeroplane to successfully fly in Britain and its use of pioneering technology such as a stepped float to reduce water drag, would pave the way for other successful designs too.

Developments begun at Windermere would later form the basis of the Royal Naval Air Service in the First World War; who used floatplanes and flying boats for coastal reconnaissance. They in turn led to perhaps the most elegant sea planes ever built, the Short Empire flying boats of the 1930s, which formed the backbone of the first global air travel. Windermere would play its part again, in the Second Word War, as a base for the production of Shorts Sunderlands, a development of the Empires which played a vital role in the protection of British shores and supply routes when we were besieged by U-boats.

iThis book tells another story too. When in 2008, drawings and archive material of the original 1911 Waterbird came to light, it became the catalyst for another project every bit as inspirational as the Edwardian original. This book, as well as outlining past history, tells the story of how a small team worked together combining modern airworthiness standards with rediscovered past craftsmanship to create an authentic recreation of the 1911 original.

Steve Slater (Ed Hicks)

It is a truly fascinating story, resulting in 2022, in a Waterbird flying above Windermere's waters once again. The story isn't over either. It is hopefully but a step on the way to a potentially more permanent exhibition which will allow the 'new' Waterbird to tell the tale of great British endeavour, which began in the heart of the Lake District.

Hats off to the pioneers from both centuries!

Stephen Slater MBE
CEO, the Light Aircraft Association.

PREFACE

I have thoroughly enjoyed writing this book with Anne Hughes.

My favourite quote about flight from water is by Captain Edward Wakefield: "Something that beckoned." His brother Arthur was a member of the 1922 Mount Everest expedition which included George Mallory. It reminds me of the phrase about climbing Everest by Mallory: "Because it's there."

I will never meet any of the wonderful characters from 1909-1919, but it has been a great privilege to reminisce with some of their descendants.

In the world today for the era since 1911, airworthy original, restoration and replica seaplanes comprise only an original 1929 Hamilton Metalplane H-47 in the USA, an original 1935 Caproni Ca.100 in Italy and the replica Waterbird. I am looking forward to

Ian Gee in the Aviat Husky

May when members of Aero Club Como will visit, including the owner of the Caproni.

The Objects of the Project are not only for flights of an airworthy replica of Waterbird but also for a Seaplane Heritage Centre on the shore of Windermere. One down, one to go ...

Ian Gee

*An aerial vew of Waterbird taxiing ***

CONTENTS

WATERBIRD'S WINDERMERE
A contemporary OS map of locations linked to Waterbird

Cockshott

Hill of Oaks

*Reproduced with the permission of
the National Library of Scotland*

PART I

As the last of the autumn leaves fluttered into the gentle waters of Windermere on the morning of 25th November 1911, those who lived and worked around Windermere were unaware that the events of the day would be a milestone in the history of British aviation.

On 24th November, Herbert Stanley Adams, a young pilot, had arranged to arrive early the next morning at the hangar which was positioned on the water's edge down a long, winding track through the trees at Hill of Oaks. The weather looked promising for a maiden flight and Adams arrived just after daybreak on the 25th November where he met Arthur Borwick who was ready to prepare the Avro Curtiss hydro-aeroplane, later known as 'Waterbird', for flight.

Frank Herbert opened his photographic studio in Lake Road near the piers at Bowness-on-Windermere not knowing that the next few days would provide unrivalled photo opportunities which could result in his pictures reaching Fleet Street. The camera with its glass half plates and tripod was ready for any eventuality and as a fine day dawned he kept an eye on the lake, where two hydro-aeroplanes had been tested over recent weeks, for eventual flights.

In Kendal, Captain Edward Wakefield was ever hopeful that his floatplane, Waterbird, was nearing her first flight from his hangar at Hill of Oaks. He knew that to be the first to have a successful flight would not only be significant for Windermere but would reserve him a place in the history of British aviation and would be the culmination of all his work and dreams – the first successful flight of any hydro-aeroplane in Britain.

Windermere from The Jetty Museum. (AH)

SETTING THE SCENE

When crowds had assembled at Kitty Hawk, North Carolina to witness the first successful powered flight of the Wright Brothers in 1903, it would have been beyond imagination to think that some of those watching would also witness, through the medium of television, the first steps of an astronaut on the moon. Sixty-six years later, Neil Armstrong's immortal words as he left his flying machine, "That's one small step for a man, one giant leap for mankind!" echoed around the world.

Any 'first' in history is well recorded, and aviation firsts included flights in hot air balloons which began to grace the skies of the Lake District in the early 1800's. In the nineteenth century, as people started to realise the dream of seeing earth from a bird's eye view, the colourful balloons became an attraction across the country, followed by early gliders launched from a rope to a car or even a cantering horse. Unpowered flying with wings became enviable but what were the possibilities of powered flight? The Wright brothers were among many experimenting with this idea on both sides of the Atlantic.

In America, Glenn Curtiss was a motorcycle manufacturer in the early 1900's, setting speed records on two wheels. Fascinated by the opportunities in aviation, he joined forces with Alexander Graham Bell's Aerial Experiment Association and in 1908 the first public flight of more than one kilometre was made in their 'June Bug' winning the Scientific American Trophy. Two years later was another first for Curtiss when his Model D aeroplane made the first take-off from a ship. It was hardly surprising that Curtiss decided to join the race to design a hydro-aeroplane that could take off and land, without mishap, on water.

Glenn Curtiss

The race was on and after several unsuccessful attempts, and many experiments with floats and engine types, Curtiss tried to take off from the surface of Lake Leuca at Hammondsport in 1908, with a 20-30hp engine, in his hydro-aeroplane now re-named 'The Loon'. The float refused to leave from the water so he returned to the drawing board.

Meanwhile on the Seine, in France, Blériot towed his water glider with a motor boat producing some embarrassing moments, captured on film, as his invention cavorted along the river, out of control. Across the Atlantic, Curtiss tried again with a new float design, this time a single float. In January 1911 he succeeded.

Curtiss had achieved a first practical successful flight status in America, but it was Henri Fabre at Martigues in France who, on 28th March 1910, who made the first successful flight in the world of a hydro-aeroplane to take off from water. He used a Gnome engine for his flight but discontinued his involvement with aircraft, later becoming little known as an innovator in the world of aviation.

Around the world, plans were drawn and experiments were made both with the design of the hydro-aeroplane and the type of engine best suited. The challenge was to improve on the Fabre and Curtiss designs

Glenn Curtiss hydro-aeroplane at San Diego Bay

and attention invariably centred on the type of float required to 'unstick' the craft from the water but also to return it with a dignified landing which did damage to neither pilot nor his transport.

A LOCAL CONNECTION

In England, a gentleman from Kendal also took up the challenge.

Captain Edward W. Wakefield came from a well-established family in Kendal with early relatives recorded as living in the local area from the seventeenth century. Born in 1862 into a Quaker family involved in municipal affairs in Kendal, Edward was to become a prominent member of the community. The family home was Stricklandgate House, known as Bank House in Kendal, and Edward

Henri Fabre – hydravion at Monaco

followed his family into banking on graduating from Cambridge University. The family owned land in the area but, rather than managing the estate and following a career in banking, Edward decided to opt for a more adventurous life. By now the family had become members of the Anglican church as their involvement in the manufacture of gunpowder was at odds with Quaker beliefs, and Edward volunteered for active service in the army. He became an officer in the Volunteer Militia Company of the Border Regiment, who were engaged in fighting in the Boer War, and he joined them in Africa.

While on leave and back in England, Edward was inducted as High Sherriff of Westmorland and after a second term of service in Africa he came back to Kendal in 1902. Still restless and with boundless energy, he made further visits abroad until finding satisfaction in the developing world of aviation. His experiences as a Captain in the army had impressed on him the importance of scouting to identify the position of enemy forces. He concluded that seeing where the enemy was from the air had distinct advantages and he decided to attend the Blackpool Air Display in 1909 in order to see a variety of aircraft in action.

He probably had not predicted that this would prove to be a turning point in his life. However, he witnessed several accidents including Hubert Latham's Antoinette and Henri Rougier's Voisin. In a letter to his wife on 19th October 1909 Edward Wakefield wrote,

"Dearest It came on wet about 4.30 today, but before that we had seen some flying and some accidents but luckily no aviator was hurt. First Roe flew in his

Captain Edward Wakefield

Blackpool Aviation Week Programme 1909

Bulls Eye a short distance then his transmission chain jammed..."

Along with his friends Rev. Sidney Swann, who was a pilot and a member of the Aero Club, and Oscar Gnosspelius, he enjoyed the air show but came to the conclusion that it could be far safer for pilots to fly from water than from land where the many obstacles on

THE LANCASHIRE AERO CLUB.

PRESIDENT: THE EARL OF LONSDALE.

TELEPHONE,
270 BLACKPOOL.

TELEGRAMS,
"AERO, BLACKPOOL."

NEAREST STATION,
SOUTH SHORE.

THE CLUB HOUSE,
BLACKPOOL.

19 Oct. 1909

Dearest
It came on wet
about 4.30 today, but
before that we had seen
some flying + some accidents
but luckily no aviator
was hurt.
First Roe flew in his
Bulls Eye a short distance.
Then his transmission
chain jammed.
Next Latham flew about
1½ miles when his engine
a beautiful 8 cylinder Antoinette

Edward Wakefield's letter to his wife, Mary

Avro triplane Bull's-Eye flown at Blackpool 1909

the ground on landing resulted in unnecessary serious injury or even fatality.

The following year, Edward identified an area on his estate which he deemed suitable to set up a hangar along the shoreline from where a hydro-aeroplane could be launched. Unfortunately, the area he chose, appropriately named Hill of Oaks, involved a steep path through a rocky and wooded area from the road between Bowness-on-Windermere and Newby Bridge. He set about clearing the mile-long track to the lake side and then built the hangar and a wet dock.

At this point in history, the success of the first hydro-aeroplane flight in France was seen as a turning point in aviation and Edward was aware of the progress Glenn Curtiss had made in America. He would no longer be able to lay claim to a world first as regards a successful flight from water, but he was eager to join in the competition to be the first to make a successful flight in Britain.

However, Edward's friend Oscar Gnosspelius, was not only building a floatplane on

Hill of Oaks in 1912 – photo from Waterhen

Windermere, as he had shared Edward's enthusiasm in the project, but had every intention of claiming the first flight in his own aircraft.

Oscar Gnosspelius, was born in Liverpool, of Swedish descent, and, as a civil engineer he had travelled to South America, Africa and Sweden as well as working in London. He lived at Silverholme, Graythwaite on the south-west shore of Windermere and, having attended the Blackpool meeting on the same day as Edward Wakefield, and, sharing Wakefield's vision, he set about designing an aeroplane that could take off from water. Having worked at a boat-builders in Arnside as a turner and fitter he had the skills for building his own aircraft.

In July 1910, Gnosspelius designed floats for his hydro-aeroplane which were constructed at Borwick's in Bowness-on-Windermere and were unique in that they included a 'step'.

Oscar Gnosspelius

Gnosspelius tested them out at Rawlinson Nab and decided that one float would be a more practical design than two. Gnosspelius used designs from early aircraft with Bleriot's design for the wings and an open lattice work fuselage from the Avro design.

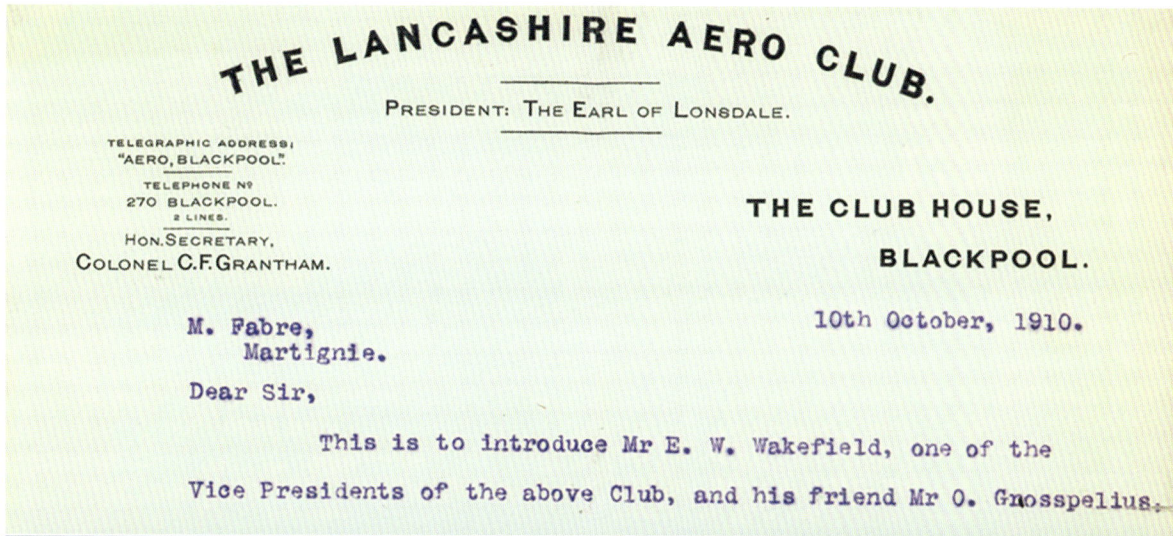

Introductory letter of Edward Wakefield and Oscar Gnosspelius to Henri Fabre

Edward Wakefield's advertisements in Flight magazine for an Aeroplane and engine

Gnome engine as used in Waterbird (IG)

Gnosspelius and Wakefield set off for France in October 1910 to visit Henri Fabre and to see his 'hydravion' which was on display in Paris and doubtless to discuss their upgraded design plans with him. In February 1911 Gnosspelius visited Brooklands where he took flying lessons with his instructor, Howard Pixton, in preparation for a straight and level flight later in the year.

A BEGINNING FOR WATERBIRD

On 1st March 1910, Edward Wakefield was elected a member of the Royal Aero Club, proposed by Rev. Sidney Swann. Wakefield also became a vice-president of the Lancashire Aero Club, based at Blackpool, whose President was the Earl of Lonsdale. The door was open for Wakefield to pursue his dream of building and flying a hydro-aeroplane on Windermere. Having built his hangar at Hill of Oaks he commissioned A.V. Roe and Company (Avro) to build Waterbird. Originally Wakefield had decided to use a Bleriot-type monoplane design for £100 (£15,000 today) but when news came of Curtiss' successful flight in January 1911 in his biplane, Wakefield and Roe decided it was going to prove more beneficial to spend an extra £150 on the airframe and to use a second hand Gnome Omega 50hp engine for which he paid £375. The surviving drawings of Waterbird show an amended design of the

Curtiss biplane described on the drawings as 'Amended design for Curtiss Biplane.'

Waterbird was first constructed at Avro's facility in Ancoats, Manchester at their workshop in the basement of Brownsfield Mills. Waterbird was an Avro Curtiss-type aircraft. It was built with the centre section made of ash linked to the canard (front elevator) and tailplane by bamboo outriggers. The wings had a wooden framework and were covered in linen. The single-seat aircraft was first built as a landplane and on completion in May 1911 was dismantled, brought up from the basement and lifted on to a horse and cart to be taken by road to the railway station. There it was loaded and transported by steam train down to Brooklands near Weybridge. This was a hazardous procedure as loads transported in this way were liable to catch fire en route, as happened in mid-July 1910 when a Roe III triplane was set alight between Wigan and Preston due to sparks from the engine.

A FIRST FLIGHT

Brooklands is well known as a motor racing track but it was also one of Britain's first aerodromes built in 1907. Names well known in aviation such as Alliott Verdon Roe and Thomas Sopwith were based there and eventually Brooklands became a major centre for flying and aircraft manufacture. Following public flying displays in 1909, flying schools were established, one by the Bristol Aeroplane Company in 1910. At this time Brooklands was described by Howard Pixton, Brookland's chief flying instructor, as comprising two dozen hangars, with earth floors and wood and canvas shutters, and the Blue Bird Café.

It was to this aerodrome that Wakefield's aircraft was brought for its first test flight on land. Four test pilots, Francis Conway

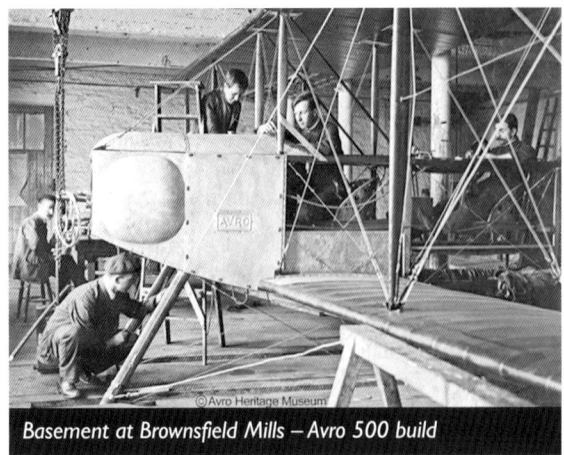
Basement at Brownsfield Mills – Avro 500 build

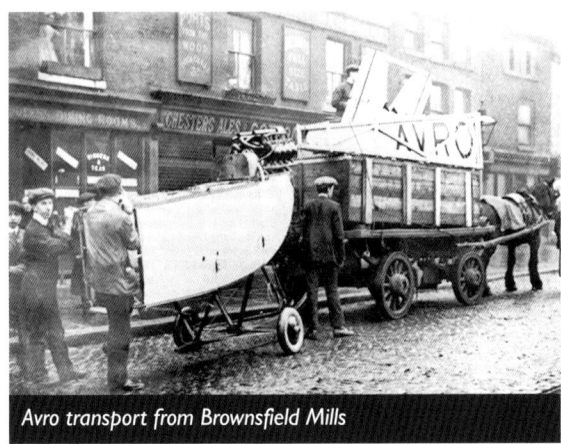
Avro transport from Brownsfield Mills

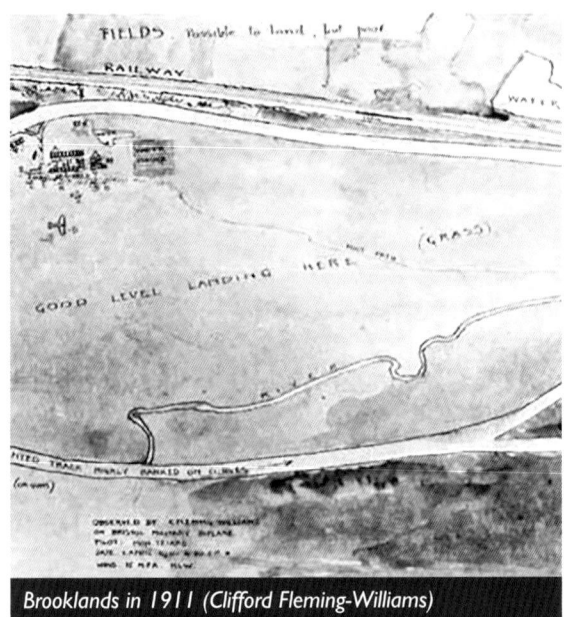
Brooklands in 1911 (Clifford Fleming-Williams)

Jenkins, Louis Noel, Ronald Kemp and Frederick Raynham were involved in flying a total of 3 circuits of the airfield. The first flight took place on 27th May 1911 and over the next six weeks modifications were made to the aircraft. The span of the upper

Brooklands (Brooklands Museum Trust)

Herbert Adams

Aviator's Certificate

wings was extended by adding another bay, the control wheel was exchanged for a column and the horizontal tail and rudder were replaced.

By the end of June, it was time for the final contract test flight and Wakefield wrote to his wife on 1st July 1911,

"At about 8 p.m. under young [he was 17] Mr. Raynham's skilful piloting a splendid flight took Brooklands by storm. Rising slowly and turning at first in wide sweeps she soon gathered speed and height and sailed for some miles (4 at least) over houses and trees, and then landed in front of her hangar as gently as a thistledown. Thus she passed her contract test with flying colours."

Wakefield now had his flying machine ready for the design and fitting of a float, replacing the wheels, so that his hydro-aeroplane could make its mark on Windermere. Duly dismantled, taken to the railway station and loaded on to the train Waterbird made the journey to Windermere where it was transported by barge to the hangar at Hill of Oaks.

A Pilot for Waterbird

Wakefield had spent time at Brooklands during the period of Waterbird's test flying and modifications and while there became acquainted with Herbert Stanley Adams. Adams was undergoing flying instruction at

Brooklands at the Avro Flying School in May 1911 and obtained his Royal Aero Club Aviator's Certificate (number 97) on 27th June 1911. Pixton, the chief flying instructor, regarded him as an exceptional pilot, 'one of the best Avro pupils'. Wakefield decided to employ Adams as Waterbird's pilot and as test pilot for the forthcoming water trials on Windermere.

WATERBIRD AT HILL OF OAKS

Unfortunately for Edward Wakefield the joyous homecoming for Waterbird turned into a series of technical setbacks and fractured the relationship he had enjoyed with the aircraft's builders, Alliott and Humphrey Roe. As a trained engineer, Adams had impressed Wakefield when he spotted a crack in a cylinder of Waterbird's Gnome engine. The crack that Adams had located was symptomatic of other issues with the engine and resulted in Wakefield appointing a French engineer, Gustav Blondeau. Blondeau's report was damning as another faulty cylinder was found not to be an original Gnome part. Faults were found in the fitting of the others and the engine was taken to France to be repaired. At the Gnome Engine Company's works it was reported that the engine was not in good condition and could not be used safely. Wakefield was charged an extra £50.00 for repairs and felt that he had paid twice as much as the engine was worth when he had bought it from A.V. Roe and Company. Wakefield was involved in a two year dispute over the payment of bills as his displeasure with the work of A.V. Roe resulted in a court case.

Adams and Wakefield also discovered faults with the airframe, including cracking of the bamboo. Discussions at Hill of Oaks followed about possible damage during test

Borwick & Sons Boat Builders at Bowness-on-Windermere

Waterbird at Hill of Oaks with Adams (seated) and Wakefield (standing)

flights and the correspondence between Roe and Wakefield was far from conciliatory. The problems resulted in a delay in readying the aircraft for its transformation into a hydro-aeroplane with the fitting of the float.

A FLOAT FOR WATERBIRD

Since the earliest designs of hydro-aeroplanes, a mere three or four years before

Waterbird's central float

Wakefield's attempt, the trickiest problem in the design was the type of float that could endure travelling at speed on the water without dipping. Having achieved flight, the float would also have to be at exactly the right angle and design for a gentle landing while the wingtip floats kept the aircraft in balance and not in danger of tipping sideways or forward into the water.

Wakefield had studied the various designs and in consultation with the local boat builders, Borwick's, he commissioned, and patented, a float with a step underneath. The bottom of the float was covered in a very fine sheet, 22 gauge, of aluminium. Curtiss had continued his development of floats and Borwick's constructed a float using Curtiss' dimensions which measured 12ft in length, was 2ft wide and had a depth of 1ft. The interior was cross-braced between the quarter inch thick mahogany sides using lattice frames of silver spruce at 6 inch centres. The upper surface was covered with waterproof canvas.

Waterbird was suspended from the hangar roof while the floor was completed and Adams tried out the pilot's seat in the suspended craft when the work was ongoing. Flotation tube wingtip floats measuring 3ft in length and weighing 14lbs were also fitted to ensure stability on the water. Trials proved unsatisfactory and in early November Wakefield had a second step added which proved to encourage Waterbird to take off.

All that was needed now was a good weather window for Wakefield, Adams and Borwick to see if a safe flight could be achieved.

WATERBIRD – A HYDRO-AEROPLANE FIRST FLIGHT

Oscar Gnosspelius had maintained a friendship with Wakefield and, as Borwick's were involved in both hydro-aeroplane projects discussions were had and ideas exchanged. In 1910, Gnosspelius started the construction of the new airframe and float in Borwick's Bowness Bay sheds and completed the work in the Spring. He made several attempts to get his hydro-aeroplane to take off from the water. Various modifications were made and he even had the idea of creating a partial vacuum which would suck in air as a cushion between the hull and the water.

There is no doubt that Gnosspelius and Wakefield both wanted to be recognised as having made the first successful flight in Britain in a hydro-aeroplane. In November both had waited in separate hangars on Windermere for the right weather conditions for a first flight, with a certain degree of frustration, anticipation and excitement that they were so close to achieving their goal.

On Saturday 25th November 1911, the conditions were calm and Gnosspelius arrived at the hangar to prepare his floatplane for its first flight. Adams too had seen the forecast the night before and arrived at Hill of Oaks at dawn. Gnosspelius winched his aeroplane into the water, floating it off the trolley and, climbing into the seat, taxied around Cockshott Point. Having just passed Belle Isle his hydro-aeroplane, Gnosspelius 2, unexpectedly liifted off from the water and crabbed to the right taking Gnosspelius by surprise. He over-corrected and the port wing-tip float went into the water causing the machine to flip over on its back. Rescuers found Gnosspelius clinging to the aircraft and both were returned to dry land.

Unable to see the drama off Belle Isle, Adams and Borwick, who had filled the fuel and oil tanks the night before, moved Waterbird out of the hangar and into the water. The weather was calm with little wind and, after he had warmed up the engine, Adams signalled for Borwick to let go of the hydro-aeroplane and he taxied towards the Bowness ferry and attempted a take-off,

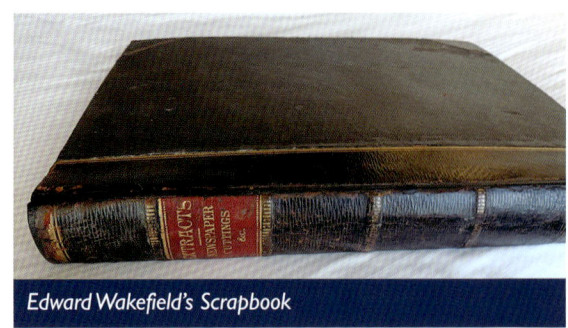

Edward Wakefield's Scrapbook

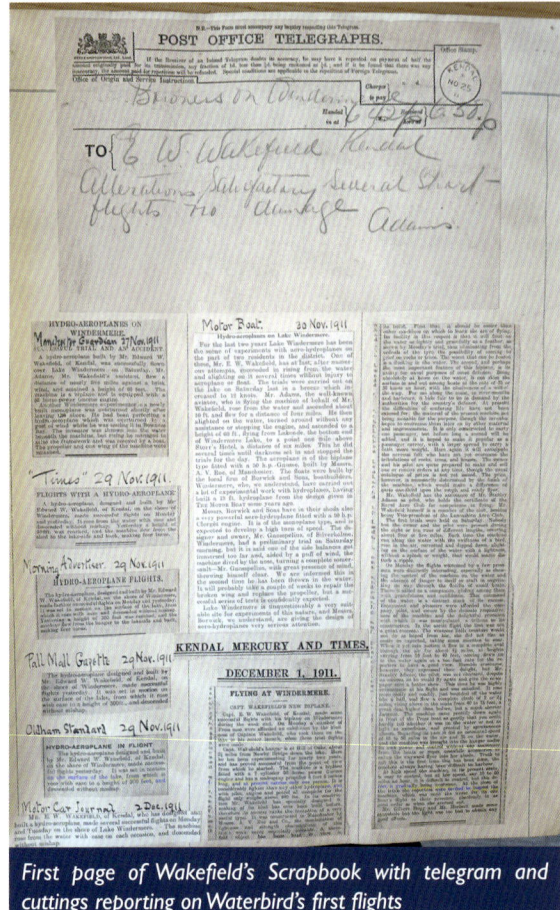

First page of Wakefield's Scrapbook with telegram and cuttings reporting on Waterbird's first flights

but Waterbird refused to do so. Adams returned, but determined to try again and now with a slight wind, he taxied once more towards Bowness ferry. After half a mile Waterbird took to the air and flew at a height of about 50 feet above the lake, made a gentle turn and returned to Hill of Oaks. Several more flights were made. At the end of the day a jubilant Adams went up to Bowness-on-Windermere and sent a telegram to Edward Wakefield announcing the success of the flights. Stamped Nov.25 1911. *'Bowness-on-Windermere 6.42pm.*

Edward Wakefield's note to his wife

Frank Herbert standing outside his shop and studio

To E.W. Wakefield Kendal. Alterations satisfactory several short flights no damage. Adams.'

Waterbird was the first British hydro-aeroplane to make a successful flight from water and to make a safe return to the water – a first for Windermere, Britain and, indeed, the Empire!

WAKEFIELD AND WATERBIRD IN THE NEWS

Fortunately for us Edward Wakefield enjoyed keeping a scrapbook! Newspaper cuttings were collected and saved as reactions to the news was reported in Fleet Street and across Britain. As the news of the achievement filtered out through the media of the day, articles were written in magazines, including *Flight, The Aeroplane* and *Motor Car Journal*. The British people from Downing Street to the North of England soon became aware of Wakefield's achievement and its implications for aviation.

In a time when it was rare for most people to possess a camera, Frank Herbert was on hand to take photos both of the hangar and on the lake during flights. Some of these photos also made their way into the newspapers and magazines. In Edwardian England Sunday was strictly observed nationally as a day of rest so no flights were

Waterbird alighting on Windermere after the second flight (F. Herbert)

19

made and newspapers were not published. The first account preserved is from the *Manchester Guardian* on Monday 27th November:

HYDRO-AEROPLANES ON WINDERMERE
SUCCESSFUL TRIAL AND AN ACCIDENT

A hydro-aeroplane built by Mr. Edward W. Wakefield, of Kendal, was successfully flown over Windermere on Saturday. Mr. Adams, Mr. Wakefield's assistant, flew a distance of nearly five miles against a brisk wind and attained a height of 60 feet. The machine is a biplane and is equipped with a 50hp Gnome engine.

Another Windermere experimenter in a newly built monoplane was overturned shortly after leaving the shore. He had been perfecting a hydro-aeroplane which was overturned by a gust of wind while he was testing it in Bowness Bay. The inventor was thrown into the water beneath the machine but rising he managed to seize the framework and was rescued by a boat. The propeller and one wing of the plane were smashed.

By Wednesday 29th November, the news had reached Fleet Street and *The Times* recorded an update of events relating to flights on Monday and Tuesday.

FLIGHTS WITH A HYDRO-AEROPLANE

'A hydro-aeroplane, designed and built by Mr. Edward W. Wakefield, of Kendal, on the shore of Windermere, made successful flights on Monday and yesterday. It rose from the water with ease and descended without mishap. Yesterday a height of 300ft was reached, and the machine flew from the shed to the lakeside and back making four turns.' Similar articles appeared in the *Morning Advertiser, the Pall Mall Gazette* and *Oldham Standard.*

Edward Wakefield was involved with the organisation of the day and travelled to Hill of Oaks to see his hydro-aeroplane in

Herbert Adams seated in Waterbird

flight for the first time. In a letter to his wife he wrote,

"Dearest,

Very best thanks for your congratulations… Today has been a great day for me. Several pressmen and photographers had gathered at Hill of Oaks so we decided to try and give them a show. It is only right Mr Adams should score his success up. She rose with some difficulty the first time and flew about 4 or 5 miles in a circle or oval at heights varying from 10 to 40 feet. Then came down like a feather without the least jar – did a mile or so to show speed and power control afloat to the

Flight magazine 27th January 1912

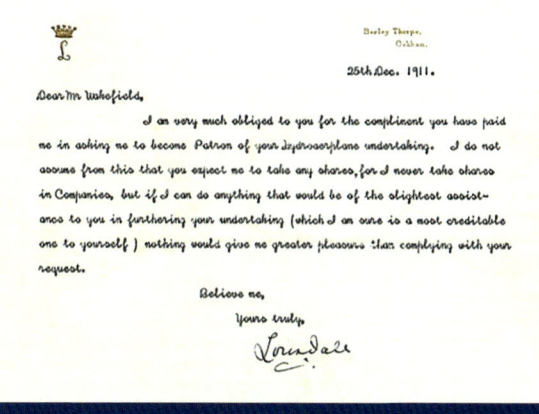

Letter from Lord Lonsdale to Edward Wakefield accepting his invitation to become Patron of the Lakes Flying Company

boats, and then up again, quite easily this time and flew another circle of some two miles at 50 miles an hour and 50 to 80 feet up. It was quite beautiful and our visitors were enthusiastic. She then returned to the hangar under her own power without being towed or aided in any way.

The engine is a treat and Adam's handling beyond praise. Not a wire was out of place but a lot of points need altering and improving and as soon as she had been well piloted we set to work dismantling for this purpose. So she can never be seen again in her first successful rig..."

On 30th November, *Motor Boat* published a detailed account stating that the 'breeze' on 25th had increased to 12 knots when Adams took off for the successful first flight and that he flew until it began to get dark. Gnosspelius' misfortune is also included here but the final paragraph makes a very positive assessment of the suitability of Windermere for flying. "Lake Windermere is unquestionably a very suitable site for experiments of this nature, and Messrs. Borwick, we understand, are giving the design of hydro-aeroplanes very serious attention."

On December 1st, the *Kendal Mercury and Times* published a feature article under the title CAPT. WAKEFIELD'S NEW BIPLANE giving a detailed and poetic description of the flights on Monday as were witnessed by 'a few pressmen' and photographers. The account mentions Waterbird negotiating its way through a flotilla of small boats 'gliding with gracefulness and confidence.' They reported on the 'delicate responsiveness' of the machine and the 'delightful precision with which it was manipulated.' The 'winsome little creature' then flew for four miles at a height of 10 to 40ft in an attempt to give the reporters a good view. Adams again took to the air in what was described as an enthusiastic flight where Waterbird 'bounded off the water like a ball, 'coming down again in front of the Press boat so gently that you could hardly tell whether it was on the water or not as light as snowflakes, and greeted by spontaneous cheers.' Reporters were then invited to inspect the machine and continued to be impressed as all was in good order.

As Wakefield and Adams, alongside Borwick's, continued to fly Waterbird and develop ideas for a two-seater hydro-aeroplane, on 20th December 1911 it was decided to form the Lakes Flying Company, originally based at Hill of Oaks, in order that flights could be given for others to enjoy the experience of flying from water. Adams was to take on the role of manager and a letter was written to the Earl of Lonsdale asking if he would consider becoming the Patron of this new venture. The Earl was well-known as one of the country's greatest sportsman but he also owned the bed of the lake which conferred certain rights. The Earl agreed and the business side of the Lakes Flying Company started to grow. Wakefield decided that operating from Cockshott would be easier and, as Borwick's had their business there, it would be beneficial to Wakefield and easier for maintenance and for the build of his second hydro-aeroplane, Waterhen. A full inventory for Hill of Oaks was compiled by Adams and completed in December 1911 and lists, among all the usual tools one would expect to find, 1 Large Hangar with adjoining workshops and storeroom; a dry dock, one hydro-aeroplane and a motor launch with tools and fittings and a skiff with two sets of oars. There is a landing stage, a wet dock, two slipways and a winch with steel cable. Also included is a weighted trolley, a large trolley and a combination forge and vice along with seven lengths of bamboo, a small float and a spare aeroplane rudder along with half a dozen

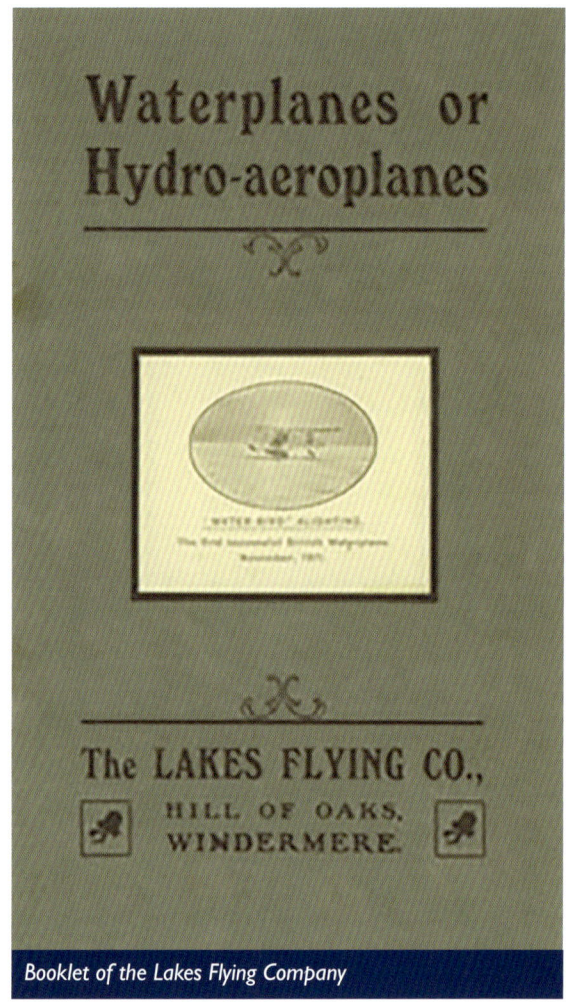

Booklet of the Lakes Flying Company

The Aeroplane magazine 25th January 1912

Waterbird in flight from Hill of Oaks (F. Herbert)

sundry pieces of 'Aluminium and Duralumin'. During 1912, aerial photos taken from Waterhen show a second hangar alongside this original hangar and much of the work on both Waterhen, and later on, the Admiralty's Deperdussin, was carried out here.

On 10th January 1912, planning permission was granted by Windermere Urban District Council. Wakefield took out a lease on land next to the lake at Cockshott where the new hangar, measuring 80ft by 44ft and painted green, was constructed with a winch-operated trolley for launch and retrieval on a ramp. The Lakes Flying Company planned to use the hangar and office for pilot training and to enable visitors to buy trial and experience flights when two-seater floatplanes were available.

A CAMPAIGN OF OBJECTIONS

However, while *Flight* and *The Aeroplane* continued to report on the achievements of Wakefield and were aware of the significance of the success of the hydro-aeroplanes, particularly for military use, Wakefield's scrapbook preserves many cuttings of a less favourable nature. Some who had grown up in the peace and splendour of the Lake District, and Windermere in particular, found the presence of aircraft flying from the lake intrusive. Letters were written to *The Times* and other publications and the local Council found itself dragged into a certain amount of controversy.

The day after Wakefield received his planning permission, a letter appeared in *The Daily News* written to the paper by Canon Hardwicke Drummond Rawnsley. Vehemently opposed to any development involving aircraft and their flights over the lake, Rawnsley had organised a protest meeting on 5th January at The Crown Hotel, Bowness and a Windermere Hydro-aeroplane Protest Committee was formed. Rawnsley's letter headed *'SPOILING A LAKE – HYDRO-AEROPLANE DANGERS AT WINDERMERE – SOME FACTS AND A PROTEST'* unsurprisingly was neither supportive of Wakefield's flights, nor complimentary. He emphasised the peace and tranquillity of the area and wrote that, not only had property prices increased because of its reputation as a restful resort, but that the business of boat building, fishing and sailing were essential ingredients in its appeal. The fear that a noisy hydro-aeroplane would instil panic into a horse or the thought that a great machine with a 50hp engine could land on visitors while they enjoyed their quiet pursuits was beyond imagination. He concluded his letter outlining alleged catastrophic scenarios which ensured his readers were well aware of the dangers of this new invention.

The following day a letter was published in *The Times* from H.B. Potter of Hill Top Farm, Sawrey. Beatrix Potter had attended the meeting and was vocal in her support of Rawnsley. In her letter she had addressed the link with the Admiralty, suggesting that these aircraft should be tested at Barrow where they tested their guns. Wakefield, she said, would monopolise the lake with his 'unwieldy machines' and although he hadn't had an accident as yet 'another aviator is fished out frequently'. The last straw was that she had heard a rumour that Wakefield's 'object is to start a local service to Rydal and Grasmere, and to carry passengers'.

Over the next week letters both in support of Wakefield and those against were published in the *Daily News*, *The Westminster Gazette* and *Manchester Guardian* including an artist from Hampstead, Henry Holliday. Holliday wrote supporting Rawnsley saying his letter 'gives us a clear idea of the injury to beauty, to comfort, to safety, and to the prosperity which will be wrought if some authority cannot be brought to bear on persons responsible for inflicting a nuisance and a danger so intolerable as that which is

Cockshott hangar rebuilt with shoring (F. Herbert)

Cockshott photo from Waterhen (F. Herbert)

imminent at Bowness on the beautiful shores of Windermere...'

There were, however, many who could see that Wakefield's enterprise could be of benefit to the area and supported him both in his flying activities and in the bringing of business to Cockshott where the new hangar was to be built. On 20 January 1912, *The Westmorland Gazette* reported on a meeting by the Trade Association in St. John's Parish Room. Mr G. S. Holland, president of the local Association said "whenever anything new had appeared there had been an outcry against it. It was so with railways, bicycles, and motor-cars; yet it had been found that the people who protested the loudest became the users and owners of the very things protested against."

The ratepayers of Bowness-on-Windermere expressed their view that the new venture would bring more visitors to the area resulting in extra trade for local residents. Towards the end of January 1912, a ratepayers' meeting was held at the Bowness Institute. The meeting was called by the Windermere Urban District Council and the following resolution was put forward: "That no difficulty be placed in the way of aeroplane development, public safety being adequately safeguarded by the powers of the Urban Council." Mr Paterson, who put forward the resolution said, "People all over the country were protesting against the hydro-aeroplane in the newspapers, but were they going to pay the rates?" He continued to say that inventors in this country were honoured as witnessed by the monuments to them in different towns and that he did not despair in seeing one in honour of Mr Wakefield. He had seen the hydro-aeroplane and saw it as a thing of

beauty and ridiculed the suggestion that a horse a mile off would run away. Another councillor, Mr Ion, made the point that the hydro-aeroplane was only an aeroplane when it was in the air and that there were no laws restricting hydro-aeroplanes which operated from the water. *The Liverpool Daily Post* reported on 25th January that the ratepayers had approved the experiments.

At the end of January, the *Manchester Guardian* reported on a meeting of the District Council who had met to discuss these issues. Landowners and residents had asked the Home Secretary to intervene and declare the lake a proscribed area. However, some councillors disagreed but an amendment was adopted with seven votes to four.

The debates continued, as did the flying, and in February the *Northern Whig* reported that Gnosspelius took to the air in his hydro-monoplane and made a successful flight of

Waterbird on ramp outside Hill of Oaks hangar

two miles along Windermere. In August, the joint official inquiry by the Home Office and the Board of Trade opened at Windermere where Wakefield conducted the case for the Lakes Flying Company. When summarised the only objections to hydro-aeroplanes were as follows:

That babies were awakened by them; that a horse may have been frightened and that a sheep had jumped into the lake on seeing one. As the last claim seemed to be the most substantial grievance the Commissioners made further inquiries as follows:

Q. The sheep was drowned?

A. No, it was not.

Q. Well at least seriously endangered and rescued with difficulty?

A. No, Westmorland sheep are good swimmers.

Q. Then what damage is alleged?

A. Well, it might have got a chill and developed pneumonia, and pneumonia is very fatal among sheep.

Q. But in fact, it did not?

A. No.

In Parliament, Winston Churchill was aware of the development of hydro-aeroplanes on Windermere and elsewhere and saw them as a necessary addition to the Royal Navy fleet. An article in *The Times* on 1st March 1912 reported that Churchill stated that 'one hydro-aeroplane was under construction at Eastchurch and that experiments with others at Sheerness, Lake Windermere and Barrow had been promising'.

Lt. Arthur Longmore and the RNAS

Churchill's involvement will have been helped by the visit of Lt. Arthur Longmore to Hill of Oaks on 20th January 1912.

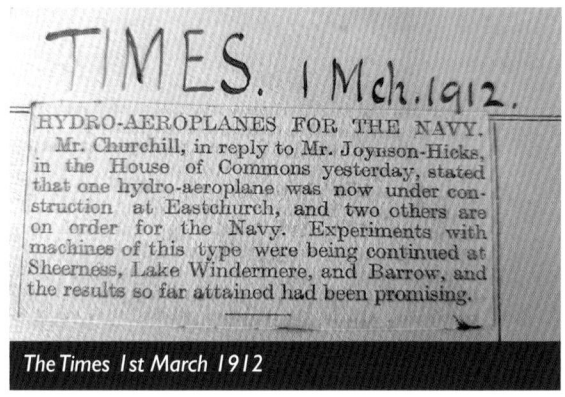

The Times 1st March 1912

Wakefield had always been convinced of the serviceability of a hydro-aeroplane for both the Navy and the Army and this was an opportunity to find out if the idea would be supported at the highest level. Longmore was sent to test-fly Waterbird for the Admiralty and to make an assessment of the airframe and its capabilities. He was one of the first four officers to be selected by the Admiralty for flying training and had achieved his Royal Aero Club Aviator's Certificate (number 72) on 25th April 1911. In 1911, Longmore had been the first person in Britain to take off from land and alight on water by fitting pneumatic flotation bags to the undercarriage skids and tail of an aircraft.

Longmore's detailed account describes a demonstration flight by Adams who, for the first time, would relinquish the seat to another pilot. Longmore was impressed with Adam's demonstration and, after an extensive and detailed inspection of the hydro-aeroplane, climbed up to the seat. Underlined in his account he wrote, 'I then took her out and had no difficulty in getting off nor landing her. I estimated she left the water at about 32 mph and that her flying speed was between 45-50... The aeroplane herself was too light and roughly made to be of much use to the Navy at the present moment but I consider that the float and undercarriage are excellent.'

Lt. Arthur Longmore

In April the Admiralty sent Longmore to Paris to the Deperdussin works to inspect the wing loading for an aircraft with the idea of converting the Deperdussin to a hydro-aeroplane. The aircraft was later delivered to Wakefield so that the necessary adaptations could be made. Two years later Longmore would find himself flying the First Lord of the Admiralty, Winston Churchill, in a seaplane at Portsmouth.

WAKEFIELD'S FLIGHT

It would be hard to imagine that Wakefield had watched his Waterbird fly and not wanted to see Windermere from the pilot's seat. Waterbird had never been designed to carry pilot and passenger with the aircraft having a restricted wing loading. However, at the beginning of February, and possibly with a certain amount of encouragement from Wakefield, Adams fitted an extra seat behind the pilot's seat and on 17th February Wakefield climbed up behind Adams. With the engine started, Waterbird taxied out and, after some time and gentle persuasion, slowly rose from the water. The flight was a few feet from the surface of the lake, then

Waterbird turned and landed as gently as possible dipping forward in the process, resulting in Waterbird, pilot and passenger being submerged. Fortunately, both occupants were rescued quickly and Borwicks later recovered Waterbird taking the sodden aircraft to the hangar at Cockshott.

The mishap was soon reported and the news coincided with Canon Rawnsley's visit to the House of Commons where he was attempting to continue his campaign to ban any flying on Windermere. Undaunted, and with Waterbird out of commission, Wakefield channelled his energy into the build of his second hydro-aeroplane, Waterhen.

WAKEFIELD AND THE ADMIRALTY

Following Lt. Longmore's visit to Hill of Oaks and his assessment of Waterbird as a hydro-aeroplane, Wakefield received a letter from Captain G.M. Paine on the subject of hydroplane floats. Paine, writing under the direction of the Admiralty, asked Wakefield to provide information regarding the price Wakefield would charge for the manufacture of floats and undercarriages for Naval machines. He also asked for an approximate cost of converting a Deperdussin monoplane, delivered to Windermere, for conversion into a hydroplane. Paine concluded by asking what amount of royalties would be required if the Admiralty adopted the floats. It was suggested that an officer would be sent to observe the construction and carry out the trials both on Windermere and at Sheerness on the open sea.

Wakefield replied that he would undertake to do the work, but without guarantee, and quoted detailed prices for the work including labour, rent of the shed, slipway and windlass fitting. Royalties would be £10.00 per float and £10.00 per undercarriage. Paine had also said that the machine would need to be able to take off from land as well as water. On 14th March, the Admiralty accepted Wakefield's terms and conditions. The Deperdussin, having been checked out by Longmore, was delivered to Windermere by train and barge on 5th June. A month later, the float now in place, the Deperdussin was ready to start taxiing trials. On 11th July Adams took the monoplane for successful test flights from the water and work for the Admiralty had begun in earnest.

THE COCKSHOTT DISASTER

The new hangar at Cockshott had worked well for Wakefield and he was able to store Waterbird there along with aeroplane parts for other aircraft, including his second floatplane, Waterhen. However, on the night of 29th March 1912, a strong wind blew up and the hangar was lifted briefly and moved away from its base, collapsing in an undignified heap and causing irreparable damage to the hangar and its contents. Early the next morning, Arthur and John Borwick arrived, having checked their boathouses to find no damage there, but a scene of devastation confronted them at the Lakes Flying Company's hangar as it became immediately obvious that the roof had collapsed on top of Waterbird. Wakefield and Adams arrived to check through the debris and soon realised that Waterbird was beyond repair. Only the canard, main float, wing section and engine survived.

On closer inspection Adams and Wakefield discovered that, where the fabric had torn, they could see that the airframe had not been constructed as they had been led to understand. Steel had been used for the box

Waterhen at Cockshott with two young passengers

spars instead of brass. Holes had also been drilled through the main spars which had weakened them. Fortunately, the fuselage and Gnome engine had been protected by the rounded roof and they were also relieved to see that the engine that had just been delivered for Waterhen was undamaged.

Wakefield's immediate reaction was to order the rebuilding of the hangar and it was later re-erected with the benefit of shoring. It is possible that the land was too soft to support the original building and that it had consequently not been secured to the piles firmly enough to resist such weather conditions.

There was no sympathy for the Lakes Flying Company from the opposition led by Canon Rawnsley, but on 16th April the government announced that aviation would not be prohibited on Windermere and that tests would continue on the lake. Wakefield went back to Hill of Oaks with Adams to fulfil his agreement with the Admiralty, supported in the House of Commons by Winston Churchill. Meanwhile, the inquiry continued.

WATERBIRD – THE LEGACY

It is amazing to consider that within the space of two years not only would a hydro-aeroplane be designed, built and flown from a small waterside hangar in the Lake

District, but that this would be the beginning of seaplanes in Britain. Windermere and Wakefield would be at the centre of invention, innovation and controversy with eventual support from Westminster. Wakefield was responsible for adapting an aircraft for the Navy which would become a necessity for the RNAS in a war in 1914.

Wakefield was also continuing the development of a two-seater hydro-aeroplane which would play a part in his commercial enterprise on Windermere, offering flights to those who had the money. He was aware that, in order to train pilots to fly from water, two seats were a necessity.

Waterhen was already undergoing construction when the Cockshott hangar disaster took place and the project was brought down to Hill of Oaks to be completed. This time the ailerons had straight trailing edges. In other respects, the hydro-aeroplane used a similar design to Waterbird but had a wider single stepped float. The passenger would be seated behind the pilot and at a slightly higher level. Not only would this give an opportunity for

visitors to the lake to enjoy aerial views but, for the few who were in possession of cameras, a chance to use the photos for promotional as well as personal use. Waterhen first took to the air on 30th April with Adams at the controls and made a successful flight.

Unsurprisingly, after Adams had taken Waterhen into the air again on 5th May 1912, Wakefield climbed into the rear seat and enjoyed his first flight over Windermere without getting a ducking! Wakefield's descriptive, and at times poetic, account was published in *Flight* magazine. He wrote, 'The beautiful outlines of the hills and mountains to the North shone through a pale golden haze with their spring greens and clear greys and russet browns growing clearer as the eye sank to the middle distance.' He also talks of men's journey from land to water who 'now go forward from water to pathways in the air, for the thing rocking on the ripples is a hydro-aeroplane – the new Waterhen'. After John Borwick swung the propeller and they took off from the lake, he said, 'The sweet air begins to sing in the wires.' All too soon the flight came to an end with a gentle landing

Cockshott hangar collapse (F. Herbert)

29

at Hill of Oaks but Wakefield was so inspired by his flight that he asked Adams to teach him to fly, discovering later that it was not as easy as it appeared!

Gnosspelius, who had never flown Waterbird, was also offered a flight in Waterhen on the same day. He had been instrumental in the design of Waterhen and was working closely with Wakefield at Hill of Oaks. Following on from this initial success, Waterhen was now available for passenger flights.

An early potential customer, Herbert à Brassard, was staying at the Old England Hotel in Bowness-on-Windermere at the end of May, having driven up his 45 h.p. six-cylinder Napier. Years later he recalled the flight he eventually took in Waterhen in the Journal of the Royal Aeronautical Society. He wrote that the hydro-aeroplane was garaged in some 'rather untidy wooden sheds' only some 100 yards from the hotel. A single engine pusher propeller bi-plane on one central float flew at a height of about 100 yards at 50-60 m.p.h. Having booked in for a flight, for which he paid four sovereigns, Mr Brassard was told he flew at his own risk and was seated on a 'kitchen chair' behind the pilot. He found the flight interesting and the final descent 'thrillingly speedy.'

On 15th July, Adams flew a record 80 miles in Waterhen making eleven flights and taking passengers on ten of these. One of his passengers on the day was Gertrude Bacon. Gertrude had enjoyed many aeronautical experiences and had become the first British woman to fly as a passenger. She also became a published author and recorded her experiences in her book '*Memories of Land and Sky.*' She was an accomplished balloonist and a Fellow of the Royal Astronomical Society and had already

Gertrude Bacon and Adams in Waterhen (F. Herbert)

LADY'S FLIGHT ROUND WINDERMERE IN A HYDRO-AEROPLANE.

Mr. H. Stanley Adams made a record voyage in the British hydro-aeroplane Water Hen, taking Miss Gertrude Bacon the complete circle of Windermere, a distance of some twenty-five miles. Above is a view of the lake taken during the flight by Miss Bacon, who is seen in the portrait. In the shallow parts the bottom of the lake could be clearly seen up to a height of 800ft.

Gertrude Bacon's flight (The Mirror)

contacted Wakefield expressing her interest in a flight in Waterhen. In her account of the day, she wrote that Wakefield met her off the Windermere steamer and 'whisked' her in his motor boat, Sarah, to Hill of Oaks. Having climbed into Waterhen behind Adams, she waited while the engine was reluctant to start but they then proceeded over the lake 'like a skimming bird with toes in the water... with the delicious lift with which an aeroplane becomes actually alive.' As with Wakefield, the flight ended all too soon but with all the positive publicity and Wakefield's article in *Flight* magazine for those who could afford two guineas for an

Admiralty Deperdussin – following conversion to floatplane

eight mile flight, five guineas for a circuit of the lake, the experience was enviable and proved a popular past-time for visitors.

AFTER WATERBIRD

The scene was now set for Wakefield and Gnosspelius to continue with experimental flights and designs. Wakefield's priority was his work for the Admiralty and by July the Deperdussin had been successfully converted into a hydro-aeroplane and had made test flights on Windermere. Having two seats it was also possible to fly passengers and could be used for pilot training. Gertrude Bacon had returned the day after her flight in Waterhen and was treated to a flight in the Deperdussin with Adams at the controls, becoming the first lady to fly in a hydro-monoplane. It had not been possible to rebuild Waterbird and the salvaged parts eventually found their way to

storage at the RAF museum in Stafford. They are now part of The Jetty Museum collection at Bowness-on-Windermere.

Photographs show a rebuild of Wakefield's Cockshott hangar and posters advertising The Lakes Flying Company's flights and training are eventually altered from Hill of Oaks as Adams was installed as manager of Lakes Flying Company based at Cockshott.

As building and adaptation of aircraft for water-based flying continued by Adams, Wakefield, and Gnosspelius, and the business grew, the first student pilot arrived for a lesson on 9th September 1912. Lt. John Frederick Arthur Trotter, from Somerset, a Lieutenant in the Royal Field Reserve Artillery, climbed into Waterhen behind Adams and, as Waterhen had no dual controls, Trotter had to lean over to follow Adams through. Trotter and Adams changed seats by the end of the day and Trotter made straight flights along the lake.

Trotter continued to make good progress with his flying, and, with Borwick's on hand, a small amount of damage to Waterhen owing to one or two mishaps, was quickly repaired. His progress continued and by October his proficiency allowed him to participate in the first air race over Windermere as, flying Waterhen, he raced Adams in the newly built hydro-biplane, Seabird. Trotter was awarded his RAeC Certificate on 12th November 1912 becoming the first pilot to have been taught to fly a hydro-aeroplane. In less than a year from Wakefield's success with Waterbird, the Lakes Flying Company was becoming a successful business enterprise both for private and commercial flying.

The business however was not financially viable as the hangar collapse and the purchase of Seabird along with bills for the

Lakes Flying Company Posters

The Northern Aircraft Company Ltd advertisement

indispensable support and expertise of Borwick and Sons, meant that business had not caught up with income from pleasure flights, training and a small income from the Admiralty. In February 1913 three aircraft are listed as being based on Windermere in a report listing aerodromes, flying schools and hydroplanes. These were Gnosspelius' hydro-monoplane, Waterhen, and Seabird.

In August 1914 the world slipped into war. The first hammer blow for Wakefield and the Lakes Flying Company was that Adams volunteered and the war that was supposed to be over by Christmas was dragging on. Wakefield was anxious to replace Adams as quickly as possible for the continuation of the business of the Lakes Flying Company. Fortuitously, and following a short article in *Flight* magazine, he was contacted by a pilot called William Rowland Ding who had logged 10,000 miles including flying

passengers in his Handley Page biplane. The aircraft was requisitioned by the RNAS in September. He described himself as a chief designer to the Grahame-White Aviation Company at Hendon. As enquiries were still being received at Cockshott from young men who were keen to learn to fly in order to join the Royal Flying Corps, Wakefield offered Ding £20.00 for a month's trial and Ding accepted.

Wakefield also decided to volunteer for active service and discontinue his involvement on Windermere. Ding had been involved with the newly-formed Northern Aircraft Company Ltd and an offer was made, and accepted, by Wakefield on 11th November 1914, to buy the Lakes Flying Company and all its assets, including the three hydro-aeroplanes, the lease on the Cockshott hangar and an option on Hill of Oaks, for £2,550. William Ding became

1915 'Flying Lesson by Moonlight' by Clifford Fleming-Williams

idea of any machine really flying was laughed out of court."

The boy, whose favourite toys were cardboard aeroplanes, had seen his dreams fulfilled and played a major part in civil and military aviation, commanding the respect of many and inspiring future generations to reach for the sky.

THE DIFFERENT PARTS OF WATERBIRD

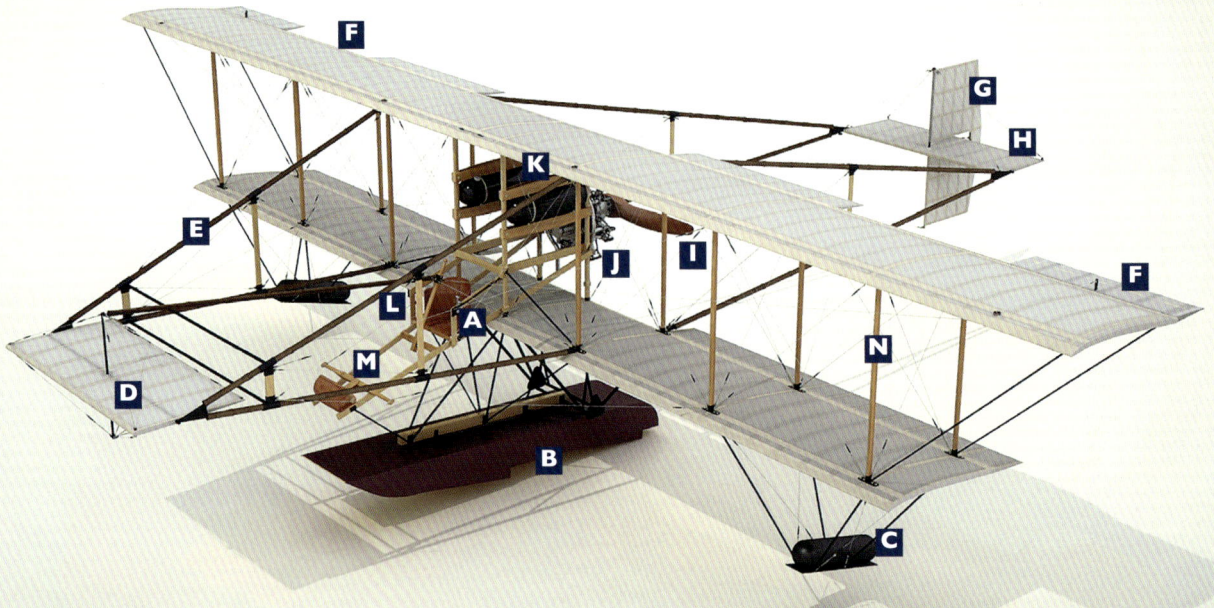

A Pilot's seat
B Main float
C Wingtip float
D Canard
E Main fuselage bamboo structure
F Ailerons
G Rudder
H Horizontal stabiliser (ground adjustable)
I Propeller
J Engine
K Fuel and Oil tanks
L Control stick
M Rudder control bar
N Wing struts

You can view a 3D fully-interactive version of this diagram at the Waterbird website:
https://www.waterbird.org.uk/replica-waterbird/

WATERBIRD SPECIFICATIONS

Length: 36 ft
Wingspan: 41 ft
Engine (Waterbird 1911):
Gnome Omega 7-cylinder
50 hp Rotary
Engine (Waterbird 2023):
Rotec R2800 7-cylinder
110 hp Radial
Top Speed: 45 mph

GNOME OMEGA ROTARY ENGINE

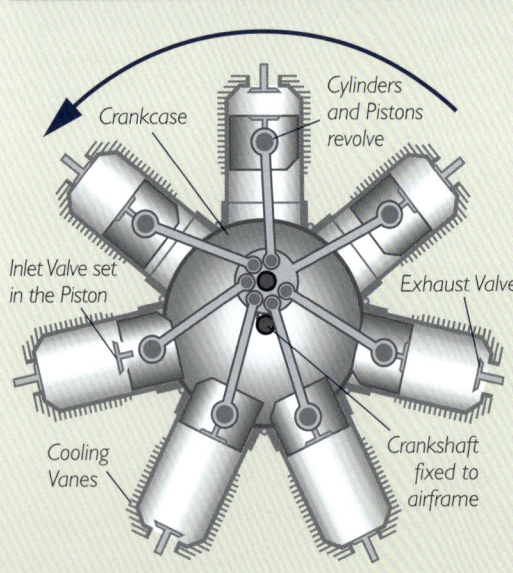

Crankcase

Cylinders and Pistons revolve

Inlet Valve set in the Piston

Exhaust Valve

Cooling Vanes

Crankshaft fixed to airframe

PART 2

The story of the events on Windermere in November 1911 has always been a part of Windermere's history, and occasional mention was made of those early days of flying in books and in articles about local history. Those with a keen interest in aviation no doubt tried to imagine the sight and sound of those frail machines operating on the lake in Edwardian England. Some will have grasped the significance of the achievement of Britain's first successful hydro-aeroplane flying from the Lake District's largest lake.

There were detailed references in some books, notably by Peter Connon in 1982,

when quotations we have included in Part 1 from the national press of the day expressed the excitement of the achievement by many, and shared the doubts of others, as to whether or not this was really needed in such peaceful surroundings.

As the milestone of 100 years drew close, those with a nostalgia for early years found their imagination stretched, as the only aircraft regularly visiting Windermere were, and still are, the fast jets of the RAF. At this time some new material from the Wakefield archive came to light in the form of some original drawings of the Avro-Curtiss Waterbird. Those who had attempted to

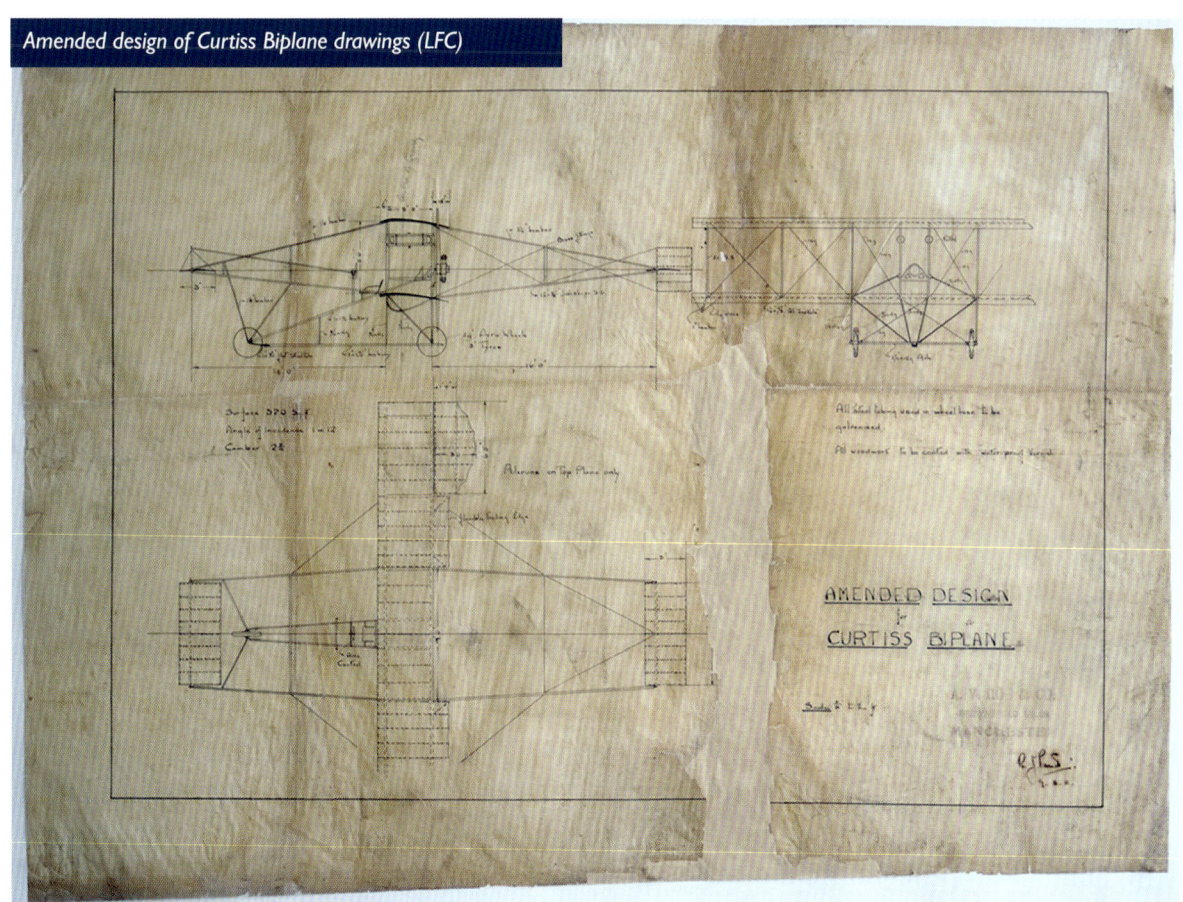

Amended design of Curtiss Biplane drawings (LFC)

imagine the events of 1911, so soon after the Wright brothers' first successful powered flight in 1903, now dared to dream, or even suggest, that a replica of the early hydroplane could possibly be built. A report was written in 2008 by Richard Raynsford, the great, great nephew of Edward Wakefield who commissioned Waterbird, in the *Westmorland Gazette* daring to make such a suggestion, and it caught the eye of Ian Gee.

Ian had grown up locally and, following the family tradition, practiced law as a solicitor in Lancaster. Ian has a passion for aviation and was awarded his wings in 1979 when he qualified as a pilot. Ian also had an interest in the history of Windermere and its stories of aviation from 1911 through to the days of the Sunderland Flying Boat base and factory at White Cross Bay. On reading the article about the drawings, Ian too started to dream that for people to see this frail machine recreated would encourage a greater understanding of the significance of this 'first' in British aviation.

In 2009, the Lakes Flying Company was re-born as the 'Lakes Flying Company Ltd' and a plan to bring like-minded aviation enthusiasts on board was set in motion. The dream became a challenge and Ian joined the group as a Trustee. The LFC Ltd took on charitable status in order that funds could be raised to see the dream of building a Waterbird replica become a reality.

The information that Richard Raynsford had found was invaluable for the project. Original drawings and accounts of the build of the Avro-Curtiss hydro-aeroplane, both from personal communications and newspaper articles, along with the original float, had brought the project credibility. Roger Mallinson made a model and also gave tuition to two students to each make a model.

Waterbird's original rudder – the oldest surviving part carrying the legend A.V.Roe & Co (LFC)

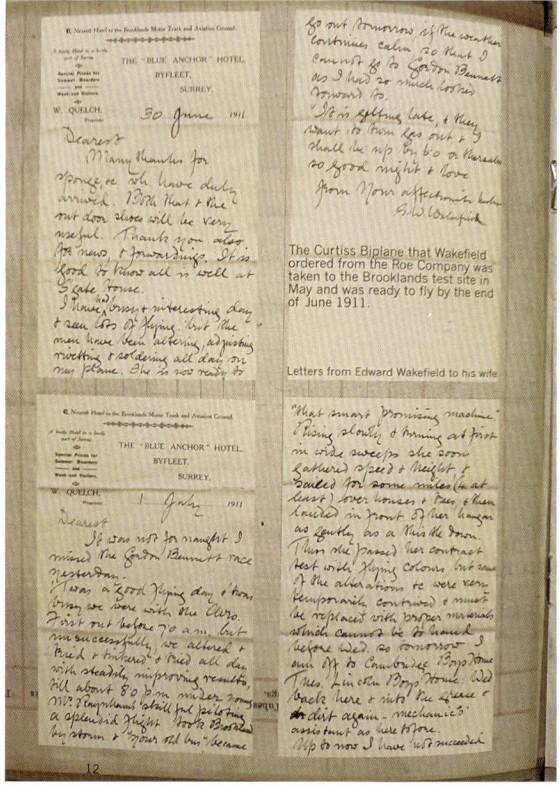

The Curtiss Biplane that Wakefield ordered from the Roe Company was taken to the Brooklands test site in May and was ready to fly by the end of June 1911.

Letters from Edward Wakefield to his wife

However, building an aircraft that remains static and is purely a museum piece is complicated but not beyond the bounds of possibility. There is also the question of funding and finding a builder who would be prepared to accept such a challenge. In the twenty first century building an aircraft that can fly requires, as one would anticipate, detailed inspections, reports, and approvals from the Civil Aviation Authority. To

Model of Waterbird (IG)

convince the CAA and insurers that this is a safe way to go requires determination and a mind-set that says that if it was done 100 years ago it can certainly be done now!

THE BIRTH OF THE REPLICA

In 2010, the Lakes Flying Company Ltd commissioned Gerry Cooper at Vintage Skunk Works hangar, Wickenby Airfield, Lincolnshire, to take on the build of the replica of the 1911 Waterbird. The challenge would be to build an aircraft that was faithful to the original construction while meeting modern health and safety regulations.

The project would be based on the 1911 drawings and inspection of the surviving original parts which were held at the RAF Museum Reserve Collection. Research was also done at the Curtiss Museum, Hammondsport, the Smithsonian Institute, and information from Practical Aeronautics. Photos of Waterbird that had been taken on

Windermere in 1911 and 1912 were carefully scrutinised. Information regarding the original materials used, Douglas fir for the main spars and solid spruce ribs bolted to the spar with aluminium cap strips, gave a guide as to choices of material for the replica. It was originally decided that aluminium tubes would be used for the outriggers but, following stress tests conducted by John Tempest for the CAA, bamboo, which had been used for the original construction, proved to be as strong and totally adequate for the build. It was also found that 'speckled' bamboo was strongest and, this being the only aircraft using bamboo in construction, an item on the pilot's checklist had to include pre-flight inspection of the bamboo for cracks.

Unusually, Waterbird had large 'elephant ears', ailerons, on the top wings. As this was very much a part of the original visual feature of the aircraft, it was decided that these would be part of the replica design but

Experimental category. This very detailed report made assessments of every part of the aircraft including stress analysis of the wings, all the cross-bracing wires used in construction, the interplane struts and fuselage and tail booms. Mathematical calculations were made and the centre of gravity estimated according to weight and balance. John's assessment concluded that the construction should be elevated to meet modern standards, and the project would now involve the Light Aircraft Association as it moved forward, before the team put the fabric on the wings.

Following a risk assessment and an overview of the project, the LAA's chief engineer, Francis Donaldson, visited the hangar at Wickenby. To say that the original 1911 Waterbird was a unique aircraft / hydro-aeroplane is an understatement, but in the twenty first century not only did the replica stand alone in the world of vintage aircraft, but presented challenges to the builders and inspectors alike. As with any prototype restoration, staying true to the original design is complicated as modifications were made in 1911 on a regular basis as a better way of doing things made sense. Waterbird flew for more than 60 hours in 1911/12, so the team knew that this replica, with all the modern technical support available, should fly and still maintain the visual impact of those Edwardian days. The LAA agreed to oversee the project and the work proceeded.

Waterbird had been operated in 1911 using a 50hp Gnome rotary engine. Barely powerful enough at the time, and hardly practical for the replica, it was decided that a Rotec R2800 would be better-suited. This seven-cylinder 2800cc radial engine would not be unlike the Gnome visually but, with 110hp, would certainly have enough power. The engine, when fitted, would have a

Instrument binnacle (John Tempest)

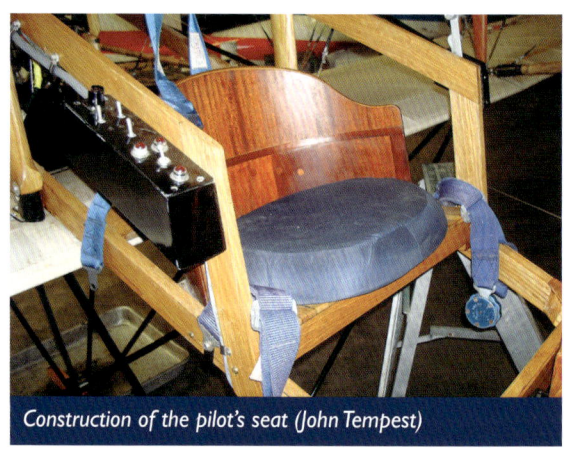

Construction of the pilot's seat (John Tempest)

Engine installation (John Tempest)

conventional throttle control, rather than a 'blip' switch, and a purpose-built Hercules

Cabane general photo (John Tempest)

Forward bamboo outrigger with turnbuckles (John Tempest)

propeller. The engine was bought from the manufacturer in Australia and shipped over to Wickenby.

The 1911 landplane had been built along the designs of Glenn Curtiss where the pilot perched on a wooden seat with engine close behind him. Comfort was never intended to be part of the design, and the pilot also required a certain amount of agility to climb up into the seat without dislodging bracing wires. It was now Mike Sales who used his skills to construct a shaped wooden seat to the dimensions and design of the 1911 biplane as far as could be ascertained. The basic instrument dials were alongside the wooden rudder bar by the pilot's feet, so good eyesight was needed to read the instruments and a wooden stick would then control the ailerons. The original had no instruments fitted but, in the replica, airspeed indicator and oil pressure instruments were installed. A fuel tank and an oil tank were positioned behind the pilot as he sat amidst a construction of wood, fabric and bamboo along with a network of wires. As with the whole build it was important to be true to the original as far as possible, but safety features needed to be incorporated before the aircraft would be permitted to fly.

Gerry and his wife, Jenny, then set about covering the wings with Diatex fabric. The width of Waterbird's wings had been extended at Brooklands by five feet and the total measurement was forty-one feet. There were four wings to cover and the fabric had to be measured, cut and laid over each wing before being glued, taped and then stretched. As Gerry used the tape and adhesive, Jenny hand-sewed the fabric using blanket stitch to ensure it remained taut. This was in preparation for applying the

Wing outbracing (John Tempest)

eight coats of dope, a lacquer used to tighten and stiffen the fabric.

When the wings were ready and the brackets in place, the moment of truth came as all hands were needed to fix the wings into place on the fuselage. Turnbuckles were in place to tension the 200 metres of cable which would take the weight both when the replica was on the ground and in the air.

LIFT OFF

It was always the plan to attach an undercarriage and wheels to the replica before attempting any water trials. In 1911, the original Avro-Curtiss Waterbird designed aircraft had been taken down to Brooklands for test flights from the grass runway to check that the design was successful and that the aircraft would fly. Fortunately for the team, Wickenby Airfield was ideal for a test flight and in 2015, when the replica was assembled and inspected, with undercarriage and wheels, Gerry

First flight – on wheels **

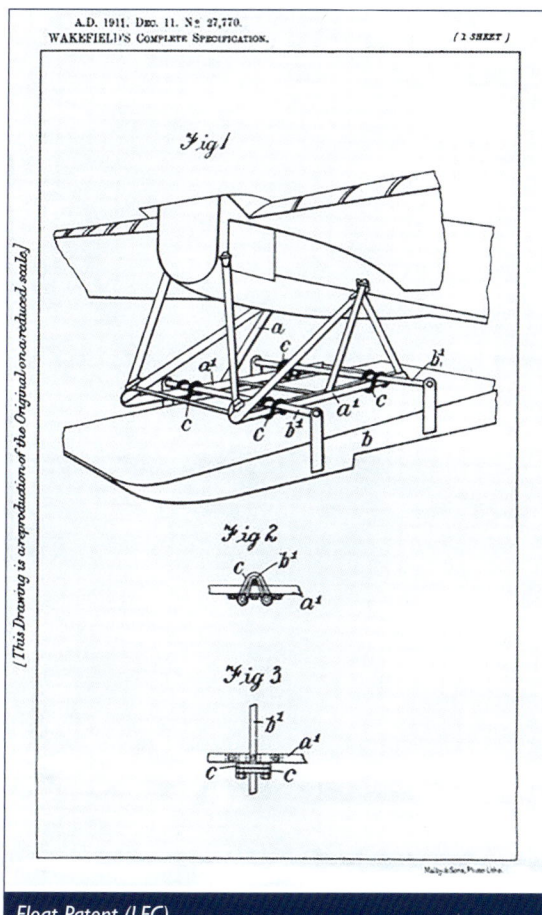

Float Patent (LFC)

Original float at RAF Museum Reserve Collection, Stafford, showing the two steps (IG)

flight of the replica Waterbird on wheels. In July 2017 the authorisation arrived and the team prepared for a first flight.

In 2018, with perfect conditions and in view of the cameras, Gerry taxied out and Waterbird left the ground up to an altitude of ten feet for short flights across the airfield. As he returned, the relief of the team and pride in the success of this unique project was evident on the faces of those who were fortunate to see the culmination of years of work. It was now time to convert Waterbird into a floatplane.

THE FLOAT

While the replica was coming together at Wickenby, a float constructed by Richard and James Pierce of Ambleside, had been brought up to Wickenby by Ian and Adrian

Cooper climbed up to his seat ready for the replica's first ground trial. Initial problems with the engine caused a delay and a further inspection was required before a permit could be issued.

When the inspection had been completed, an application was made to the Light Aircraft Association for a 'Permit to Test' for a test

James Pierce at work on the float *

together with a specially-designed trailer, which would be used to launch and recover the floatplane. The float had been designed using computer software and, as far as possible, using measurements from the original drawings. In 1971, surviving parts, including the original float, had been donated to the RAF Museum and the team had located the float to help in the design process.

In 1911, experiments were made using various designs of floats for hydro-aeroplanes and although the aircraft would float on the water outside the hangar it was another matter for it to depart from the water as the pilot attempted to take off. Those who did manage to take off, then found it was another challenge to land on the water without capsizing.

Edward Wakefield had decided that the float would need a 'step' underneath to encourage a departure from water and, having made trials on Windermere with his design, he added a second step which he then patented. Wakefield's patented stepped float was a world first! The original float had survived

and was a great help in the design of the replica float. The replica float would need to have the same visual impact as the original but also produce the required lift.

Following the successful flights at Wickenby, Gerry started on the conversion which involved cutting the keel and putting on the additional metalwork to connect to the float.

In order for Waterbird to be flown as a floatplane, rather than a landplane, and because changes had been made to the structure of the aircraft, it was necessary that further tests and analysis were made. Cranfield University MSc students provided the necessary calculations and two reports were made by them.

In 2020, the team took Waterbird to the National Water Sports Centre in Nottingham's Holme Pierrepont Country Park for a first launch. It very quickly became apparent that there were serious problems resulting in Waterbird being removed from the water before any damage to the aircraft was sustained. The test had

Waterbird testing the float at the National Watersports Centre, Nottingham *

Examining the first float *

shown that the size of the replica's float lacked reserve buoyancy.

This time, and with the work at Wickenby completed, Waterbird was dismantled, loaded on to a low-loader, and taken to a new home at Liverpool's John Lennon Airport. To see the frail machine journeying across to the M6 and travelling along the local roads into the airport was not a sight for the fainthearted, and the team who had been involved over the last ten years, were relieved that Waterbird had arrived safely.

FIXING THE FLOAT PROBLEM

Engineer Dr.William Brooks now took on the role as the 'Competent Person' for E

Conditions. This time, another local boat builder, Hamish Patterson from Hawkshead, built the second float with Naval Architect Jack Gifford as designer. Naval Architect Prof. Paul Wrobel, acted as the Lakes Flying Company's overseer of the project. The replica's float was now transformed with a 22 gauge aluminium floor, five watertight compartments and the rigid wingtip floats had three watertight compartments.

Before any more trials were to take place, another detailed report had to be made and submitted to the LAA. Bill Brooks undertook this work, along with John Wighton of Acroflight Ltd who made a full assessment of the aircraft and its capabilities. This included a calculation of the crosswind component and maximum weight of a pilot, 95kg. Because of the limited lateral and directional control, a limit of 20 degrees bank must not be exceeded. The CAA had also agreed that the registration G-WBRD need not be displayed on the aircraft with the only wording 'LAKES FLYING COMPANY' on the rudder clearly visible and

Waterbird's arrival at Grubbins Point *

Unloading the centre section in the rain *

braces, turnbuckles, fittings and the bamboo in preparation for a scrutiny of the float and a launch the following day.

THE PILOT

Pete Kynsey is a test pilot, well known in aviation circles for flying and displaying warbirds, including Spitfires, at air shows. By contrast, his intricate aerobatic display

Bill Brooks (It should fly like this!) *

Pete Kynsey demonstrates the controls (AH)

flight in the diminutive Cosmic Wind, the 'Ballerina,' is a masterpiece of sensitive flying. Pete's flying career started with instructing and he moved on with helicopters, air taxis and private jets to airliners. He also enjoyed competition aerobatics, and flying vintage aircraft. Ski flying in the high Alps is another interest but currently Pete's Aviat Husky on floats gives him the opportunity to instruct would-be floatplane pilots in the south of England. Pete was approached and asked if he would be happy to test-fly Waterbird and he agreed.

ON THE LAKE

This was not an occasion for the public to see Waterbird in action, so very few people around Windermere were aware of the significant events at Grubbins Point.

First trial 2021. At the jetty. *

Taxi (Roger Lane)

Hamish alters the second float after the porpoising problem*

Supported by a rescue boat, Pete started the engine and taxied away from the shore. He gradually increased the power. There was relief that at last the replica was level and making progress but, at five knots below take-off speed of thirty knots the floatplane began to porpoise on the water. Several attempts were made to reach take-off speed, and it became apparent that all was not well. Waterbird returned to the launch site for

Ready for a second attempt. June 2022. Bill Brooks attaches weights to correct the centre of gravity*

Francis Donaldson (LAA) *

another consultation with the engineers. After discussion it was decided to return Waterbird to Liverpool and for modifications to be made. As a result, the design of the underside of the main float was altered and the angle of attack between the aeroplane and the main float was increased.

RETURN FOR A FIRST FLIGHT FROM WATER

In 1994/95, a public inquiry took place concerning the imposing of a byelaw on the lake that there should be a speed limit of 10 knots. The Lake District National Park Authority has the power to grant permission to exceed this limit by way of an exemption application process. The take-off speed of the Waterbird replica is 30 knots, so for any flight the application must be approved. Other boxes had to be ticked as for a public flying display including the appointment of a Flight Display Director, in this case Charles Sunter, to oversee all the safety issues around the flight. A rescue boat with diver, Lake Rangers' and Lake Wardens' boats were in place on the day, following notification to lake users that the flights would be made on the lake at a specific time.

In June 2022 Waterbird made a second journey from Liverpool to Grubbins Point where the team, this time accompanied by Francis Donaldson the LAA's chief engineer, were waiting in anticipation of a re-creation of the day in 1911 when Waterbird first took to the air. Francis had prepared the LAA's permission for the flight to take place and, after inspecting the replica, the' Certificate of Clearance' was issued on site. This was not a public flight and, although all the procedures and permissions for a flight had been cleared with the CAA and the Park Authority, very few were aware that this was

Pete Kynsey ready for flight *

Taxi for flight *

to be a significant day in the history of the replica. However, the Warplane Workshop TV crew had been preparing a documentary for *More4* to be shown later in the year and were on hand to film the day, whatever the outcome. Pete Kynsey would eventually say that he saw this as a 'fantastic project and he couldn't wait to take the aircraft into the air' (*Westmoreland Gazette* June 2022), but

at this point, as Waterbird was untried and untested in the air, he approached the flight with a little trepidation.

The next day it was necessary to see if, with the modifications to the float, Waterbird would settle comfortably in the water. Once released from the trailer and supported on each wing tip by two of the team in waders, the replica was slowly brought to the jetty

Her first flight. (Francis Donaldson)

and human ballast, in the form of Adrian Legge, climbed from the jetty into the pilot's seat. With engineers on hand, various small adjustments were suggested and when Waterbird returned to the hangar these were made in preparation for the trial first flight.

Pete is the ideal test pilot to be given the opportunity to make history again on Windermere and the challenge of flying this replica of a 1911 hydro-aeroplane was irresistible. The first challenge, having conducted the pre-flight checks including inspecting the bamboo outriggers, was to get into the pilot's wooden seat. By standing on the jetty and climbing along the float, Pete was able to climb over the struts and wires and, having donned flying suit and life jacket, he settled into the seat. Pete then put on his flying helmet, goggles and seat belt and was ready for Waterbird to be turned by

The replica Waterbird makes her first flights. (Mark Wright)

Aerial shot of the return to the hangar *

the team, still in waders, who had supported the replica while Pete embarked.

As the engine started up and Pete taxied out to the lake the team waited in anticipation as the RIB boat, with the Flying Display Director aboard, accompanied the replica. Waterbird gathered speed, leaving the water

without difficulty for a first 'hop'. All was well and Pete continued his straight-line planned take-offs and landings returning to the team who had witnessed another 'first' for Windermere and the reward of years of dedicated work. Waterbird, G-WBRD, was rewarded with the LAA's 'Permit to Fly' and

The replica Waterbird makes her first flights. (Mark Wright)

September 2022. A return to Grubbins Point for a first public flight (AH)

was officially on the books as the latest airworthy floatplane. Fortunately, one or two local photographers were on hand to provide the team with photographic momentos of the day, echoing those archive photos taken in 1911 by Frank Herbert.

Pete's experience and observations were appreciated as flying this unique aircraft required great skill, as it had with the Edwardian Waterbird when Herbert Adams flew on Windermere in 1911.

The team having celebrated the occasion, the following day Waterbird was dismantled, loaded up and made for a return journey to Liverpool. The temporary hangar was then removed and the quiet bay left as it had been found for water activities to resume.

A PUBLIC FLIGHT

Plans were now drawn up for a very public occasion on Windermere where press and public would be invited to witness Waterbird flying. Arrangements had to be made and permissions granted by the Park Authority and the CAA, as again all ferry operators and boat owners would need to be notified about the replica's flight. Notice was issued to civilian pilots and the RAF were informed as regards low flying activities. Two days in September were chosen to give the team an option of flying on either day as it was just possible that weather conditions would not be perfect for flying on both days. A time slot of two hours each day was nominated as all were notified as to the arrangements, including local and regional press, TV and the Press Association.

This time there was no need for secrecy, so personal invitations were issued to many of those who had been involved in the project and to relatives of the early pioneers who designed, built or flew Waterbird.

In Liverpool, Waterbird was once more dismantled and loaded up before the nail-biting return journey to Windermere along the M6. Once again the temporary hangar

A wet start. Visitors arrive by boat to see the replica Waterbird (AH)

had been erected and the lorries negotiated the winding track down to the water's edge. With Waterbird safely in the hangar, Bill Brooks was on hand to check every cable, turnbuckle, nut and bolt as well as a careful check of the bamboo which had previously developed a minor crack owing to the climate-controlled conditions in the Liverpool hangar. Bill Brooks had bound the crack and then continued a careful inspection of the engine and float before announcing that all was in order!

On 22nd September, the first day planned for a flight, the morning TV news programme reported the planned flight for the day. The news was followed by a dismal weather forecast and a brief look out of the window showed that it looked very unlikely that flying could take place. Later in the morning, reporters and TV crews arrived at the hangar to make plans for their reports, realising that it would be the following day, with a forecast for perfect conditions, when they would need to make a return journey. Pete Kynsey climbed up to the pilot's seat and demonstrated the use of the controls for the reporters, who had made an early start in anticipation of a busy day.

The guests had been invited to gather at 'Broad Leys', by courtesy of the Windermere Motor Boat Racing Club, and the plan had been that they would transfer by boat to the hangar, to have a close view of Waterbird, after Waterbird's flight. As the rain fell and mist formed over the lake it was decided to erect gazebos by the hangar as the guests would require shelter on arrival. In the afternoon, with the flight cancelled for the day, boats delivered the group, some in Edwardian attire and equipped with umbrellas, for their first view of this remarkable machine. At 41 feet wide and 37 feet long many were amazed at the size and work involved in the re-construction of this first British hydro-aeroplane from over 111 years ago.

When all were assembled, the President of the Lakes Flying Company, Sir Benjamin Bathurst GCB DL, (retired) Admiral of the Fleet, addressed the group. Sir Benjamin, who had a personal connection to the Wakefield family, talked about the fragility of those early aircraft and the bravery of those who flew them. He stressed how they had shown resistance, patience and imagination and that seeing the replica

The next day – Waterbird wheeled out of the hangar into the sunshine (AH)

LAKES
FLYING
COMPANY

Waterbird in her birthplace proved a poignant experience. His speech was followed by a response by Rear Admiral Tom Cunningham. Paul Wrobel explained how the next part of the plan was to find a permanent base on Windermere where replica Waterbird would be the centrepiece. Ian Gee concluded the formalities saying it had been "a thrilling opportunity to step back in history to the very earliest days of aviation, when pioneers pushed the boundaries of what was possible through innovation and imagination".

As the rain cleared, the group boarded the boats for a return trip across the lake and made plans to revisit Windermere the following day to witness Waterbird in flight.

The 23rd September dawned fair and conditions for flying were ideal. In the hangar, reporters had returned and checks were again completed. A final round of tea and sandwiches were enjoyed by the team, and Charles Sunter held a full briefing in readiness for the flight. Several of the

visitors, who had attended the event the day before, also joined the group at the hangar to relive the scene of over one hundred years ago.

The team were well-rehearsed for the launch, having dressed in waders and wet suits, and all watched as Waterbird G-WBRD was slowly manoeuvred out of the hangar and hitched up to the tow car for the careful transfer into the water. At the water's edge, Pete climbed up to take his seat.

The tow car continued to reverse into the water as the team supported the wings and slowly the replica Waterbird floated off the trailer. All onlookers watched with relief as the replica settled on the water, looking completely at home in this environment. The RIB boat had arrived for Charles Sunter, along with Ian Gee, to be ready to escort the floatplane and support boat as Lake Rangers spoke with one or two curious sailors who had failed to read the briefings! Looking a little vulnerable on the lake, the replica Waterbird suddenly came to life as the

Kate Tripp and Adrian Legge turn Waterbird ready for the engine start-up (AH)

engine started. Cheers were heard from the bankside from all who had committed to the project over the years, and members of the families whose relations had built and flown the 1911 Waterbird. The replica taxied out into the water and along the lake, accompanied by the support RIB boat.

As Waterbird took to the air, more cheers could be heard around the lake, where crowds had assembled, while a moment of history was re-created. After four 'hops', she taxied back and Pete's smile was apparent as he turned into the bay and the team waded out to bring her in and re-install her in the hangar.

It was the culmination of years of work, overcoming the many problems of any

Bringing the trailer into the water (AH)

Taxiing out on to the lake (AH)

The BBC capture Waterbird's flight

Waterbird (Martin Dodgson)

Waterbird (Martin Dodgson)

aircraft replica or restoration build, and the team deserved the pride they experienced as Waterbird was brought back inside. In the evening, local television news covered the story and a star was born!

In the next few days, the replica was dismantled, loaded up and the journey back to Liverpool reinforced the team's determination to find a permanent home on Windermere so that everyone could enjoy seeing Waterbird and discover the story surrounding this unique aircraft.

AN ARTY DAY

As the new year began, a group of aviation artists from the Guild of Aviation Artists were invited to spend a day at the hangar in

The Team (photo from June flight)*

Sketch from the day (Phil Hadley)

Liverpool. Phil Hadley and the Midland GAvA group, journeyed up equipped with art materials, easels and chairs, and were met with a challenge for the day. None had seen Waterbird before and all were amazed at the intricacies of the design and the complicated structure. As Phil would say later, everyone present had managed to capture the essence of the Waterbird with some very keen and accurate observation being carried out. The

64

The GAvA Midland Group turn up for a sketching day at Liverpool (AH)

Another sketch from the day (Vince Nevin)

mediums used varied from pencil crayons to watercolour to line and wash, acrylic and oils.

The Guild artists produced sketches which were admired by onlookers and demonstrated the feel of the environment around the flights many others had been fortunate enough to witness.

JUST THE BEGINNING....

By definition an aeroplane is a flying machine that moves from one place to another through the air. However, Waterbird, and the Waterbird replica have parallel histories in that both have travelled extensively by rail or road.

By the time you read this book, there will have been another journey up the motorway from Liverpool to Windermere, this time to Rayrigg Wyke. In order to be transported it is necessary for the aircraft to be dismantled and re-assembled. After each journey engineers are on site to inspect every part, wire and strut and only after it has passed inspection can Waterbird be launched again. Meanwhile, the Lakes Flying Company Ltd continue to look for a permanent site to establish a Seaplane Heritage Centre on the shore of Windermere where visitors will see her for themselves and she can make regular flights. This will be the legacy which will inspire the young enthusiasts of today to look to the future of aviation on land and water, with visions of new designs for the 21st century and beyond.

Preparing to fly at the jetty *

Waterbird at home on Windermere (Ray Troll)

LAKES
FLYING
COMPANY

POSTSCRIPT

THE BOOK

The challenge and privilege of writing a book telling the story of both the original and replica Waterbird proved to be irresistible! For Part 1, where we tell the story from 1909 of Edward Wakefield's dream to build a hydro-aeroplane, we were fortunate to have an archive of material, centering mainly on Wakefield's dedicated collection of newspaper cuttings in his scrapbook. As he was an avid letter writer, we were allowed a peep into his private life with preserved letters to his wife. The Lakes Flying Company also own the original drawings, now held in Kendal's Archive, and a small selection of Frank Herbert's published photographs. Along with all of that, there are a few preserved surviving parts from the original aircraft.

In Part 2, the build of the replica had been over a number of years and in two locations. There again we are grateful to Ian Cundall, of *Air TV*, for allowing us to use photos from the TV programme *Warplane Workshop* and to *Primetime Media* who gave us access to the *Warbird Workshop* film made earlier. There were also documents from the reports, giving us far more technical information than we could include in the book. We were fortunate too in the

The Book – Putting the finishing touches to our book! (AH)

generosity of local photographers who between them had produced an archive of material as they photographed Waterbird on the three occasions she visited the lake.

As we proceeded with writing the book, the characters of the early days started to come alive in our imaginations and we hope that we have succeeded in bringing them back to life for our readers.

Anne Hughes and the AHUK Robert Pleming Memorial Award for G-AVDF 2021 (Tim Badham)

THE AUTHORS

ANNE HUGHES

Anne has written articles for many publications as a freelance writer. A former pilot, flying light aircraft, and volunteer researcher at IWM Duxford, most of her published work is in the world of aviation and she has been a monthly columnist for the Light Aircraft Association's magazine for six years as well as having articles published in aviation magazines and publications. Formerly editor of the Beagle Pup and Bulldog Club's magazine, *Beagle News*, she is currently Chair of the Vintage Aircraft Club and a trustee for the National Transport Trust and the Lakes Flying Company Ltd.

Her first published book, *G-AVDF – The Beagle Pup Prototype, Return to the Skies* – written jointly with Andy Amor, tells the story of another significant and unique aircraft for which she oversaw the six year project for restoration to flight. Awarded for her work with the LAA and VAC with the Royal Aero Club's Certificate of Merit she has always been aware of the privilege of working in aviation.

IAN GEE

Ian's dedication to the build of the replica Waterbird is unrivalled, and his love of history, in particular the history of aviation, is second to none. Ian has inspired the

12-year project and acted as Chairman of the trustees of the Lakes Flying Company Ltd. He has made a significant contribution to the replica's journey to flight both in time and financially.

Ian has also provided his time and enthusiasm for recording the story in a way that would encourage the reader to enjoy comparing the world of 1911 on Windermere with that of today. Ian's dedication to preserving the story for future generations also extends to the work he puts into the flying days, the care of Waterbird while she is out of public sight and articles, talks and interviews. His plans for the future of this remarkable aircraft are a vision that is shared by all involved.

Ian enjoys flying floatplanes but has no plans to climb up into Waterbird's seat!

WATERBIRD PROJECT AWARDS

Since the replica took to the air, awards have been forthcoming from several organisations in the world of aviation.

In 2022 and 2023 Ian Gee and the Waterbird team have received the following:

National Transport Trust – Bremont Special Recognition Award

Aviation Heritage UK – Robert Pleming Memorial Award for Innovation

Ian Gee accepts the Desmond Penrose Silver Salver VAC Award for 'Aeroplane of the Year' from Desmond Penrose! (Tim Badham)

The Aviation Heritage UK Robert Pleming Memorial Award 2022 for innovation (IG)

Vintage Aircraft Club – Desmond Penrose Silver Salver Award, Vintage Aeroplane of the Year

Royal Aero Club – The Salomons Trophy.

PUBLISHED ARTICLES:

Several articles about the build and flights of Waterbird have been published.

The Light Aircraft Association's *Light Aviation* – 2018, 2022, 2023 by Ian Gee, Francis Donaldson and Anne Hughes

Flight Deck Magazine – 2022 - by Ian Gee

Royal Aero Club on-line Winter 2022 newsletter – by Anne Hughes

Aeroplane Monthly December 2022 edition – by Ben Dunnell

The Flying Machine (Press Release)

Pilot magazine December 2022 edition – by Peter March/Anne Hughes

National Transport Trust Winter edition – by Anne Hughes

Air Pilot December 2022 edition – by Anne Hughes.

We are grateful to the staff of Castle Green Hotel, Kendal and The Wheatsheaf Inn, Brigsteer, who provided us with room to set up and work on the book on many occasions in the comfort of their establishments.

Lastly we would like to thank Trevor Jago for the lay-out and printing of this book, and for his time, patience and encouragement in working with us!

Waterbird (Martin Dodgson)

FACEBOOK

Over the last few months we have set up a new Facebook page for Waterbird, *Waterbird – Wings over Windermere*. At this point in time we have over 150 members and have enjoyed sharing photos from the 1911/12 life of Waterbird and up-to-date news of events.

We will continue to use this media as one way of raising awareness of the project as it proceeds, and encouraging a growing local group of followers.

WEBSITE

Our website, *www.waterbird.org.uk* is regularly updated and provides detailed information on the history of Waterbird as well as administrative matters and contact details. There is an interactive model of the replica on the website as well as technical information. The Lakes Flying Company is a registered charity and details regarding donations are included.

Waterbird – Wings over Windermere event poster 2022 (Design – Katie Housmone)

QUOTES...

'To fly over water is certainly to taste to the full the joy of flight, and when the water is Windermere and the scenery the pick of English Lakeland, which is to many a traveller the pick of the whole world, in its soft intimate loveliness, the result is something not lightly forgotten.' –

Memories of Land and Sky by Gertrude Bacon

'It was Captain Wakefield's Waterbird which made the first successful flight in 1911 and Windermere thus gave birth to the age of the Seaplane.' –

The Great Age of Steam on Windermere by G H Pattinson

'The great tradition of innovation and successfully overcoming the severe and unique difficulties in operating aircraft on water all stemmed back to Waterbird and the pioneering designs and spirit that she represented.' –

Navy Wings

The first aerial photograph of Windermere (F. Herbert)

'Edward Wakefield's ideas were scorned, but he never lost faith in the hydro-aeroplane, and Waterbird was a successful expression of that faith.' –
Historic Military Aircraft by J M Bruce

'The combined efforts of aviators, ship and boat builders-turned aircraft manufacturers at Barrow-in-Furness and Windermere during 1908-1914 justify the area's claim to be the birthplace of British Naval and civil marine aviation.' –
Triplane to Typhoon by J H Longworth

By way of an introduction to the book Aeromarine Origins, H F King, MBE formerly editor of Flight magazine, chose four quotations. From Sir George Cayley in 1809, Lawrence Hargrave in 1902, Dayton Daily News in 1907 and from Edward Wakefield in 1912 when he described Waterbird: '....like a fine bird, between water and sky in the changing lights.'

WINDERMERE TIMELINE

July 1910

The first aeroplane floats with a 'step' in the world were designed and tested by Oscar Gnosspelius (later Major), constructed by Borwick & Sons, on Gnosspelius No. 1. – Statutory Declaration, 11 January 1913.

9 March 1911

Captain Edward Wakefield commissioned a landplane from A. V. Roe & Company, which was constructed at Brownsfield Mills, Manchester. The drawings, dated '9.3.11.', are the oldest surviving of any Avro aeroplane.

7 July 1911

Arrival of the landplane at Windermere, having been test-flown at Brooklands, for conversion to a hydro-aeroplane and to be known as Waterbird.

The central float and wingtip floats were made by Borwicks.

25 November 1911

Gnosspelius made the second successful take-off outside France and the USA by a hydro-aeroplane/ the second successful take-off in the world with a stepped float/ the first successful take-off at Windermere, in Gnosspelius No. 2. – *The Westmorland Gazette*, 21 December 1911.

Gnosspelius No. 2 was the first British hydro-aeroplane to employ auxiliary wingtip floats. – *The History of British Aviation 1908-1914* by R D Brett.

25 November 1911

Herbert Stanley Adams (later Lieutenant Colonel) made the first successful take-off and landing outside of France and the USA by a hydro-aeroplane/ the first successful take-off and landing in the world with a stepped float/ the first successful take-off and landing at Windermere, in Waterbird. – *Kendal Mercury and Times*, 1 December 1911.

Wakefield described flying from water as "Something that beckoned...". – *Aeromarine Origins* by H F King.

20 January 1912

Lieutenant Arthur Longmore (later Air Chief Marshal Sir) was the first member of the Royal Navy to successfully take off and land a floatplane/ the first member of the Royal Navy to fly at Windermere/ the only person other than Adams to fly Waterbird, when he test-flew Waterbird for the Admiralty and compiled a Report; his arrival having been kept a secret.

23 January 1912

Rear Admiral Ernest Troubridge (later Admiral Sir), Chief of Staff, published a paper on The Development of Naval Aeroplanes. For the obtaining of personnel, he proposed 'Bristol school or Wakefield hydro-aeroplane school to train those pilots that cannot be received at Eastchurch at present'.

14 February 1912

Gnosspelius made the first successful take-off and landing in the world by a hydro-monoplane of 'normal' type/ the first in Britain by a hydro-monoplane of any type in Gnosspelius No. 2. – *The Aeroplane* magazine, 29 February 1912.

He was the only person at Windermere to design and fly his own hydro-aeroplane.

29 February 1912

Winston Churchill, then First Lord of the Admiralty, was asked in the House of Commons about hydro-aeroplanes and the Royal Navy. He replied by referring to experiments, including at Windermere, and that "the results so far attained have been promising".

29 March 1912

Waterbird was rendered beyond economic repair when the hangar collapsed at Cockshott.

60 flights on 38 different days, the furthest for 20 miles, had been accomplished and 800 feet attained. – *The Aeroplane* magazine, 25 January 1912.

16 April 1912

Churchill was asked in the House of Commons about hydro-aeroplanes at Windermere. He answered that tests would continue on the lake.

3 May 1912

The first passenger to fly at Windermere was Wakefield in Waterhen [Waterbird's successor]. – *Flight* magazine, 11 May 1912.

By the end of 1912, more than 100 fare-paying passengers had been carried in over 250 flights.

15 July 1912

Gertrude Bacon became the first woman in the world to be taken up as a passenger in a hydro-aeroplane/ the first passenger in a hydro-aeroplane to make a complete circuit of the lake, in Waterhen. – *International Women in Science* by C M C Haines.

16 July 1912

Wakefield became the first person in the world to fly as a passenger in a hydro-monoplane, an Admiralty Deperdussin. – Letter to Wakefield from Charles Grey, Editor of *The Aeroplan*e magazine, 17 July 1912.

The Deperdussin had been converted from a landplane at Windermere, in compliance with an Agreement between the Admiralty and Wakefield which was subject to the Official Secrets Act.

16 July 1912

Gertrude Bacon became the first woman in the world to fly as a passenger in a hydro-monoplane, in the Deperdussin being tested for the Admiralty. – *International Women in Science* by C M C Haines.

19 July 1912

An Admiralty representative came to Windermere to observe a new method of transmitting wireless messages from air to surface.

9 September 1912

Second Lieutenant John Trotter Royal Field Reserve Artillery, received the first lesson with the Lakes Flying Company, the first British hydro-aeroplane school.

12 September 1912

Wakefield obtained UK Patent No. 27,770 for the means of attaching a float to a hydro-aeroplane.

27 September 1912

Hill of Oaks was inspected by Lord Rayleigh, President of the Advisory Committee for Aeronautics.

12 November 1912

Trotter was granted an Aviator's Certificate by the Royal Aero Club ('RAeC') No. 360 – this image is of the RAeC's index card. Trotter was the first person/ first member of the Army to achieve a UK Certificate with tests taken on a hydro-aeroplane.

'Letter from Wakefield, of 21 February 1912, with regard to Hydro-aeroplane Certificates was read. It was unanimously resolved to grant provisional Certificates in respect of tests carried out on hydro-aeroplanes, such certificates to be subject to confirmation by the Fédération Aéronautique Internationale ('FAI')'. – Minutes of Executive Committee of the RAeC, 27 February 1912. Confirmation by the FAI was made at its Conference on 15 and 16 March 1912.

18 March 1913

Wakefield obtained UK Patent No. 27,771 for a stepped float for a hydro-aeroplane. After considerable experiment, he had combined features of construction in a novel way. – H Hatfield, Patents Judge.

12 June 1913

The only occasion when a Windermere-based hydro-aeroplane operated outside of the Lake District, save for flights in 1919 to/from the Isle of Man. Having been transported by traction engine, Waterhen was flown by Adams at Hornsea Mere, near the Yorkshire coast, for Hornsea Horse Show. Passengers, on the first ever flights from the Mere, were taken up at £2 a time. – *Hull Daily Mail*, 12 June 1913.

25 August 1913

The first flight at Windermere with 2 passengers, by Adams in Waterhen.

30 August 1913

The first UK Hydro-aeroplane Certificate No. 614 was awarded to Lakes Flying Company pupil James Bland, and on 15 April 1914 the second Certificate No. 765 to Oswald Lancaster.

On 28 January 1913, Wakefield had accompanied the RAeC representatives at an Extraordinary Conference of the FAI held in Paris. 'The FAI decided that ordinary Aviators' Certificates should be valid for flights over both land and water. It was further decided that Certificates should be granted in respect of tests over water, but that such Certificates should not be valid for flights over land.' – Minutes of Executive Committee of the RAeC, 4 February 1913.

Also at that Conference, the Schneider Trophy for an annual international seaplane contest was accepted and the rules passed.

13 November 1913

Wakefield obtained UK Patent No. 18,051 for a float of a seaplane to support its own weight during flight.

12 February 1914

Gnosspelius obtained UK Patent No. 10,801 for a V shaped float. This gave a sharper angle, reduced drag and was advantageous for structural reasons and for aerial considerations.

The V shape is used on almost every float manufactured today.

22 January 1915

Flying tuition by moonlight (drawing by Clifford Fleming-Williams (later Major) was a record. – *The Aeroplane* magazine, 27 January 1915.

21 October 1915

The first seaplane (Waterhen) to alight on Esthwaite Water, flown by John Lankester Parker with pupil John Coats.

18 March 1916

The first seaplane (Blackburn Improved Type 1) to alight on Coniston Water. This photo was taken back at Windermere of Henry Reid standing in the front cockpit and Parker behind. – *Blackburn Aircraft since 1909* by A J Jackson.

May 1916

The school was taken over by the Government, so that training operations at Cockshott and Hill of Oaks became Royal Naval Air Service Unit Hill of Oaks.

3 June 1916

The headquarters of the RNAS at Windermere moved from Cockshott to Hill of Oaks, and, with the departure of civilian instructors, the name was changed to RNAS Windermere.

19 July 1916

RNAS Windermere was inspected by the First Sea Lord, Sir Henry Jackson.

July 1916

Shortly after discharge from hospital, Flight Lieutenant James Ferrand (later Major) was posted to RNAS Windermere as an instructor, where he remained until 20 November 1916. On 28 November 1915, whilst piloting an F.B.A. off Ostend, he had attacked an Albatros seaplane accompanied by 3 more seaplanes and a destroyer. Ferrand's gunner brought down the Albatros and he then attacked the destroyer, whilst under heavy shell fire from the destroyer and shore batteries. It was the first time that a seaplane had shot down another. For this action, he was awarded the Distinguished Service Order.

20 May 1917

On 20 May 1917, 2 ex-pupils, Flight Sub-Lieutenants Charles Morrish and Henry Boswell, were the pilots of Curtiss H-12 Large America 8663 flying boat near Flushing in the North Sea, operating under the 'Spider Web' system of searching for submarines. Bombs were dropped on a U-boat, which was 'the first submarine sunk by the Royal Naval Air Service.' – *The Royal Navy Day by Day* by L Phillips. Both were awarded the Distinguished Service Cross on 22 June 1917.

Within the same list, ex-pupil Flight Sub-Lieutenant Charles McNicholl was also awarded the DSC, for his services in convoy protection and combatting submarines whilst stationed at RNAS Dundee.

On 31 August 1917, Adams (then Squadron Commander) was awarded the DSC for services in the Eastern Mediterranean.

Flight Commander Guy Price, an instructor at Windermere November-December 1916, was awarded the DSC on 22 February 1918 and Bar on 16 March 1918 [a gap of only 22 days], an ace having downed 12 aircraft.

Flight Lieutenant John Hume began his training at Windermere in May 1915 and was posthumously awarded the DSC on 17 May 1918 for services in Mesopotamia.

June 1917

The White Ensign was lowered at RNAS Windermere.

10 May 1918

Captain Cooper Pattinson, from Windermere, whilst based at RNAS Killingholme shot down a Zeppelin over Heligoland Bight. He was awarded the Distinguished Flying Cross, amongst the first list of recipients in the London Gazette.

3 June 1918

The first list of Distinguished Flying Crosses 'gazetted' also included ex-pupils Captain Harold Gonyon, for bombing a U-boat near Dunkirk on 3 April, and Captain Victor Bessette, for services over the North Sea.

The DFC was instituted after formation of the Royal Air Force as the equivalent to the Distinguished Service Cross for acts of valour at sea: between the level of these awards and the Victoria Cross is the Distinguished Service Order.

19 July 1918

Flight Officer William Dickson's first appointment was on 11 November 1916 as a pupil at Windermere. – High Commanders of the Royal Air Force by Air Commodore H Probert. Dickson was awarded the Distinguished Service Order on 21 September 1918 for having taken part on 19 July in the first strike from an aircraft carrier (returning aircraft would have to ditch in the sea), when 7 Sopwith Camels from HMS Furious attacked airship sheds at Tondern, Denmark. The senior flying officer of Furious was Lieutenant Colonel Richard Bell Davies VC, DSO. 'The most outstandingly successful carrier operation of the war'. – *Naval Aviation in the First World War* by R D Layman. He became Marshal of the RAF Sir; the first Chief of the Air Staff to have begun his career as a Naval pilot and the last to have served in World War 1.

An attack on Tondern had been recommended by Captain Oliver Swann (later Air Vice-Marshal Sir), commanding officer of aircraft carrier HMS Campania. On 18 November 1911, he took off in an Avro D from Cavendish Dock, Barrow-in-Furness. The choice of aircraft was discussed with Longmore (then Wing Commander serving in the Admiralty Air Department) when he visited Campania.

August 1918

Borwicks were subcontracted by Dick, Kerr & Co. Ltd. of Preston to manufacture Felixstowe F.3 flying boat hulls. – *Dick, Kerr & Co. Limited A History of the Company 1853-1919* by J Shorrock.

21 July 1919

Seaplanes returned to Windermere with the arrival of an Avro 504K operated by the Avro Transport Company and flown by Howard Pixton (later Captain),with a second the following week. They were based at the Cockshott hangar. The enterprise included joyriding flights which had been pioneered by Waterhen, passenger flights, instruction and delivery of newspapers to the Isle of Man.

4 August 1919

The first flight carrying newspapers to the Isle of Man, by Pixton. *The Daily News* was overprinted in red '*Seaplane Edition*'.

8 August 1919

The first fare-paying passenger from or to the Isle of Man, flown by Pixton.

8 October 1919

The end of Avro Transport's operations at Windermere.

9 October 1933

Saunders-Roe A.19 Cloud amphibian G-ABXW, known as the Cloud of Iona, landed and anchored in The Narrows between Belle Isle and Borwicks' boatsheds, departing the following day.

11 September 1942

Parker test-flew the first Windermere-assembled Short Sunderland flying boat DP176, 26 years after he last flew at Windermere.

35 Sunderlands were built at White Cross Bay through to May 1944. In addition, 25 were repaired or converted to 1945.

3 February 1943

A Slingsby Falcon 1 water glider was flown by Pattinson, and also on 7 February by Flight Lieutenant Wavell Wakefield.

Late 1944

3 Consolidated Catalina flying boats landed in late 1944, and in the first part of 1945.

13 January 1945

The prototype Short Shetland flying boat visited.

The proposal to build 10 Shetlands at Windermere did not materialise.

13 August 1979

Tiger Moth G-AIVW landed at Low Wood Bay, departing the following day.

September 1983

A Cessna 180 amphibian came to Low Wood Bay, with a view to a business being set up for seaplane training, an air taxi service and pleasure flights.

28 June 1990

Sunderland G-BJHS, known as Islander, stayed until 17 July.

27 June 1994

Catalina G-BLSC stayed until 11 July.

13 June 2022

Replica Waterbird G-WBRD first flew, 110 years since the original last did so and 28 years since the previous seaplane at the lake.

23 September 2022

First public flight of Waterbird G-WBRD.